INNER SANCTUM

INNER SANCTUM

Memory and Meaning in Princeton's
Faculty Room at Nassau Hall

EDITED BY KARL KUSSEROW

With contributions by Toni Morrison, Sean Wilentz, Karl Kusserow,
Eddie S. Glaude Jr., and Paul Muldoon

PRINCETON UNIVERSITY ART MUSEUM

Distributed by Princeton University Press

Inner Sanctum: Memory and Meaning in Princeton's Faculty Room at Nassau Hall
is published by the Princeton University Art Museum and distributed by Princeton University Press.

Princeton University Art Museum, Princeton, New Jersey, 08544-1018
artmuseum.princeton.edu

Princeton University Press, 41 William Street
Princeton, New Jersey 08540-5237
press.princeton.edu

The book is published on the occasion of the exhibition
Inner Sanctum: Memory and Meaning in Princeton's Faculty Room at Nassau Hall,
on view in the Faculty Room from May 28 through October 30, 2010.

Inner Sanctum has been made possible by Paul and Heather Haaga, William and Christy E. Neidig,
William H. and Judith McCartin Scheide, Michael and Julia Baccash, and the Kathleen C. Sherrerd Program Fund for American Art,
in honor of the Class of 1970 on the occasion of its fortieth reunion.

Managing Editor: Jill Guthrie
Assistant Editor: Sophie Williams
Designer: Bruce Campbell
Typesetter: Mary Gladue
Printer: Meridian Printing, East Greenwich, Rhode Island, under the supervision of Daniel Frank

Library of Congress Control Number: 2010922941
ISBN: 978-0-691-14861-8

Cover and frontispiece: details of the Faculty Room at Nassau Hall

This book was typeset in Bembo and Perpetua display and printed on Scheufelen PhoeniXmotion Xantur, 115# Text.

Printed and bound in the United States of America.

Contents

For this historic project in which the Class of 1970, celebrating its fortieth reunion, has been proud to take a leading part, who better to call upon than Robert Reidy Cullinane, our "Poet Larvaeate," to express in the Class Foreword the import and purpose, from '70s point of view, of *Inner Sanctum: Memory and Meaning in Princeton's Faculty Room at Nassau Hall*. Robert has given both the Class and the University much of value by way of the written word, and not the least is the Class epigraph on '70 Plaza, never truer than today:

IN A SEASON OF UNREST
AMID THE CROSS FIRES OF THE LEFT AND RIGHT
WE FOUND HERE
IN GOTHIC HALLS AND IN THE GOODNESS OF FRIENDS
THE KEEP OF REASON
AND THE STEADYING BOND OF COMMUNITY

H. Kirk Unruh Jr., Class of 1970
Recording Secretary

Class of 1970 Foreword

With the linear preoccupations of an architect crossing his mind, Raleigh Gildersleeve felt it necessary to reassure—with some hesitation—his employer, President Wilson, in 1905: "I am glad that my designs for the alteration of Nassau Hall met with your approval. I do not feel that the oak wainscot does not have its effect, even though it is to a very large extent covered by portraits. Your hall has some very large pictures in it, and yet the feeling that the wainscot is really behind the pictures gives it richness." Looking at Princeton's Faculty Room today, so perfect a marriage of iconography and millwork that few can imagine the one without the other, who would be inclined to disagree with him?

The Class of 1970 is pleased to lend its auspices to another reimagining of the Faculty Room, but this time, after an intervening century has enshrined the space as Princeton's holy of holies, it is more in the spirit of reverence than renovation. *Inner Sanctum: Memory and Meaning in Princeton's Faculty Room at Nassau Hall* will honor the Class's fortieth reunion with, in addition to this book, an exhibition *in situ*, a fall 2010 Freshman Seminar on the linkages between art and spatial environment, a reading in Richardson Auditorium by the volume's contributors, and a student concert recreating one that was given in the room in 1762.

The heart of the college from the beginning, the small Spartan room that began as the prayer hall evolved in size, function, and name into—respectively—a Revolutionary War hospital, barracks, and prison; the state legislature; the capitol of the United States (Fitzgerald's "tribunal of early American ideals"); the college library; the Museum of Geology and Archaeology (a choice that held for twenty-four years); and today's Faculty Room, initially known as FitzRandolph Hall, a designation quickly transferred to the memorial gate. And the chamber quickly collected on its walls portraits of Princeton's royalty who would, if they could see out of their frames, no doubt be very pleased with their solemn and finely appointed setting. One frame in particular, that containing George II, was according to verifiable legend deprived by cannon shot of its occupant during Alexander Hamilton's rout of British troops, and soon held another George, the commander-in-chief of the Continental Army. This frame, along with numerous others and the paintings they hold, has been restored by the Class of 1970 in a project led by Class leaders Paul and Heather Haaga, William and Christy Eitner Neidig in memory of Lorenz E. A. Eitner, Graduate School Class of 1952, Michael and Julia

Baccash, and our honorary classmates William H. Scheide, Class of 1936, and his wife, Judith, and the late John J.F. Sherrerd, Class of 1952, and his wife, Kathleen.

As the symbol and nucleus of University authority, the Faculty Room has been and continues to be the magnet of activity of the highest consequence, the scene of great speeches, and the focus of interest to students and visitors alike. This was no less true in times of dissent as in placid eras. If a single room can represent a mighty and multifaceted university, embody its spirit, and stand for all that it encompasses, this room does. Yet it is the portraits that speak most vividly to us: the prim Dr. Burr, Nassau Hall's first president who worked himself to death in its name; Witherspoon, master of statesmen; McCosh, the fiery Scots philosopher; Wilson, who made the college into the University; and our own Goheen, clear-eyed leader in an era of change.

Members of the Class of 1970 have taken their places as trustees and debated University policy in this, Princeton's House of Commons; have consecrated it with memorial services; have resorted to it as to a sanctuary for quiet reflection and inspiration; have bestowed honors in it; and recently, in one of its more creative uses, the room was translated into a ship's quarterdeck for the retirement from the Navy of a flag officer, one of our own, who was "piped over the side." We revere it, in Woodrow Wilson's words at the dedication ceremony in 1906, as "the nursery of the nation's ideals" and "the historical center of Princeton's life."

Civic engagement, awareness of the wider world, and service to society have always characterized the Class of 1970. Forty years ago, in June 1970, commencement day reflected the tumultuous spirit of the times, manifested over four years of protest and reaction. Now we undertake the restoration of the University's most sacred relic, Peale's portrait of Washington, and sponsor an exhibition on the enduring significance of a Princeton landmark. The decades have marched on, bringing as they always do the evolution of youthful creeds, and the iconoclasts of yesteryear have become the conservators of today. The Class that opened the FitzRandolph Gates is proud to open the Faculty Room for the artistic, architectural, and historical edification of the community.

Robert R. Cullinane, Class of 1970
Office of the Recording Secretary

Foreword

Like Princeton University, this volume is a rich amalgam of the physical and the intangible; of fact and meaning; of legacy and possibility. It explores what Toni Morrison describes as "the place of the idea and the idea of the place" in the context of Princeton's institutional portrait collection and the historic chamber, known today as the Faculty Room, in which thirty-three of these paintings hang, while, at the same time, looking far beyond them.

For this is also the story of Nassau Hall, of Princeton as a whole, and of the forces and currents that have shaped our University since it moved to Princeton from Newark in 1756. Indeed, at its most expansive, *Inner Sanctum* is an exegesis of history itself and the past's inescapable bearing on the present.

Each contributor to this volume has approached his or her subject from a different angle. For Karl Kusserow, Princeton's Associate Curator of American Art, the portraits in Nassau Hall are not merely representations of eminent Princetonians; they also constitute a reification of history that "solidified Princeton's past, constructing it as linear, stable, even dynastic, when in fact it had been punctuated by periods of doubt, inactivity, and decline." His account of Princeton's portraits and their immediate environment is therefore as much about institutional self-understanding as it is about the circumstances under which the collection was assembled and displayed.

Historian Sean Wilentz traces the epic evolution of Nassau Hall, Princeton's most venerable building, from its colonial beginnings through the violence of the Revolutionary War and two disastrous nineteenth-century fires to its present iconic and administrative roles. As he points out, Nassau Hall is more than a stately edifice: "it is a battle-scarred monument to the University's—and the nation's—continuities and changes."

In his thought-provoking essay, Professor of Religion and African American Studies Eddie Glaude speaks for the men and women of color whose portraits have yet to find a place in the Faculty Room, suggesting how the burden of a wounded history can form the basis for regeneration. As he puts it, "We turn to the past . . . to better equip ourselves to invade the future intelligently, and with love."

Nobel laureate Toni Morrison invokes the "wisdom of the dead and the energy of the living" to capture the essence of an institution that is both rooted in history and visionary enough to transcend it. For her, Princeton's portrait collection, past, present, and future, documents this "balance of conservation and change, tradition and progress."

Finally, in a poem entitled "The Inner Sanctum," Paul Muldoon, the chair of Princeton's Lewis Center for the Arts, envisions the portraits lining the walls of the Faculty Room not as lifeless artifacts but as a vital force that spurs today's Princetonians to action in the world beyond our campus.

For all their individuality, the contributions to this volume form an eloquent and incisive whole that reveals how much there is to glean from the historic heart of one of America's oldest and greatest universities.

Shirley M. Tilghman
President

Preface and Acknowledgments

A portrait is a hybrid of art, identity, and history. When collections of portraits are formed by institutions, their meaning extends beyond the literal and figurative frames that contain them to embrace the history and identity of the larger entities they also thus come to represent, reflecting the institution's distinctive character even as they help shape it.

For more than a century and a half, Princeton University has presented its past and thereby a significant part of itself through portraits. Haphazardly at first, but with growing purpose and direction, the University employed portraiture to codify and embody the narrative of its history through the lives of its leaders, distinguished faculty, and select alumni, eventually amassing a collection of over four hundred portraits now displayed in more than fifty locations throughout campus. The core of the collection hangs in Nassau Hall's Faculty Room. Here are the portraits on which the collection was founded, and together with those that have joined them in the ensuing years, they create a distinct historical narrative. Their story is echoed by the room in which they are displayed, whose own multifaceted evolution mirrors Princeton's changing aims and concerns over time.

This book and the exhibition it accompanies examine the history and role of that room and the portraits within it as the symbolic center of the University, and explore the function of each in the construction and maintenance of Princeton's identity. What ultimately emerged in 1906 as today's Faculty Room, a place devoted to the display of the institution's most significant portraits, is the culmination of a long and illuminating trajectory begun only a decade after the school was founded, when Nassau Hall opened in 1756 with a prayer service in that same space. Yet when former U.S. President Grover Cleveland formally dedicated the Faculty Room one hundred fifty years later, he was in a sense completing a circle rather than providing the endpoint to a successive line of development. For the bequest that made possible the room's renovation, as well as the impressive new gate at the campus entrance in front of Nassau Hall, came from Augustus Van Wickle, whose ancestor Nathaniel FitzRandolph had in 1753 given the college the ground on which "Old North" was built. As Princeton (and future U.S.) President Woodrow Wilson said in acknowledging the donation at the Faculty Room's inauguration, "there could be no more appropriate gift from a descendant of Nathaniel FitzRandolph than one which touched with added beauty his original gift."

It is especially fitting, then, that the funding for this project comes in turn from Princeton's Class of 1970, a group with their own connection to what is now called the FitzRandolph Gate. It was they who, "in a symbol of the University's openness to the local and worldwide community," ensured upon their graduation that the formerly closed gate would always remain open to the town and the world beyond it. For their continued generosity in now making possible the opening of the refurbished Faculty Room and this book investigating its history and significance, the Museum is indeed grateful, and wishes in particular to thank Paul and Heather Haaga, William and Christy Eitner Neidig in memory of Lorenz E. A. Eitner, Graduate School Class of 1952, and Michael and Julia Baccash for their munificent support, as well as H. Kirk Unruh for his invaluable assistance in arranging it. Major support also comes from an Honorary Member of the Class, William H. Scheide, Class of 1936, and Judith McCartin Scheide, and from the Kathleen C. Sherrerd Program Fund for American Art, established by John J.F. Sherrerd, Class of 1952—also an Honorary Member of the Class of 1970.

Eloquently introduced by Princeton's president, Shirley M. Tilghman, this volume includes essays by some of the University's most illustrious faculty, whose contributions thoughtfully and fluently engage the Faculty Room and its Nassau Hall home as both place and symbol. To President Tilghman; Toni Morrison, Robert F. Goheen Professor in the Humanities, Emerita; Sean Wilentz, Sidney and Ruth Lapidus Professor in the American Revolutionary Era; Eddie S. Glaude Jr., William S. Tod Professor of Religion and African American Studies; and Paul Muldoon, Howard G.B. Clark '21 University Professor in the Humanities, we express sincere thanks for their highly valued participation.

Although the exhibition accompanying this book takes place outside the walls of the Museum, in the Faculty Room itself, the project's realization results from the talented efforts of many of my Museum colleagues, most especially Manager of Campus Collections Lisa Arcomano, Managing Editor Jill Guthrie, and Senior Preparator Michael Jacobs. Long in gestation, the project benefitted from the crucial support of three Museum directors: Susan M. Taylor, acting director Rebecca E. Sender, and current director James Christen Steward. In addition, Brice Batchelor-Hall, Michael Brew, Tracy Craig, Jeffrey Evans, Caroline Harris, Laura Lilly, Norman Muller, Karen Richter, Betsy Rosasco, Nancy Stout, Sophie Williams, and Albert Wise were particularly helpful.

Considerable research was undertaken in connection with the project, most of it impeccably carried out by Miri Kim, Graduate School Class of 2013, and Jeffrey Richmond-Moll, Class of

2010, both students in Princeton's Department of Art and Archaeology. Their contributions to my essay in particular cannot be overstated. They in turn would like to thank Ben Primer, Associate University Librarian for Rare Books and Special Collections; Julie Melby, Graphic Arts Librarian; Daniel Linke, University Archivist, and the staff of the Seeley G. Mudd Manuscript Library, especially Daniel Brennan, John DeLooper, and Eugene Pope; as well as Elizabeth Patten and Megan Peterson of the Office of Communications.

Appropriately, given the project's Princeton orientation, individuals throughout the University community assisted in various ways. From among them, special thanks to Robert Cullinane, Class of 1970, for the foreword to the book's special edition; Ruth Boatman, Nicola Knipe, and John Weeren for facilitating textual contributions; Hanne Winarsky for arranging details of the book's distribution; Ann Halliday for coordinating the Museum's temporary presence in Nassau Hall; Sandra Saccone, Christopher Gorzelnik, and Kenneth Grayson for help preparing the Faculty Room for exhibition; Thomas Roddenbery, Eloise Tomei, and Frances Yuan for initial development assistance; and John Wilmerding, Christopher Binyon Sarofim '86 Professor in American Art, Emeritus, for early support of the project.

Finally, several people beyond FitzRandolph Gate merit mention for a range of contributions, including Elizabeth Baughan and Paul Gratz for sensitive conservation of the portraits and their frames; Bruce Campbell and Bruce M. White for, respectively, this book's elegant design and photography; Carol Soltis for portrait expertise; Charles Stone, Class of 1976, for lighting expertise; and W. Barksdale Maynard, Class of 1988, for assistance and advice with my essay.

For such diverse but uniformly appreciated contributions to *Inner Sanctum*, I extend my sincere thanks. It has been my privilege to work on a project that so well articulates the nature of this University community: honoring the past, committed to the future, and above all, coming together in the present to live up to this place, this idea, that is Princeton.

Karl Kusserow
Associate Curator of American Art
Princeton University Art Museum

THE PLACE OF THE IDEA, THE IDEA OF THE PLACE

A MEDITATION ON THE FACULTY ROOM AT NASSAU HALL

TONI MORRISON

Trying to say something relevant, something original about an institution so permanently lodged in the history of higher learning and the history of the nation is a singular honor for me, but it is also a daunting assignment more easily undertaken by a policy maker than an artist. While wondering how to shape these remarks I looked through works of other writers, poets, novelists, historians, and turned at one point to William Wordsworth hoping to find suitably elegiac lines. I hoped those of us who merge our love of Princeton University with allegiance to its mission would be receptive to a meditation on genius loci—the "spirit of the place"—Wordsworth's eloquent use of the conceit that certain (natural) sites held genii which "spoke" to the contemplative passerby. Ruminating on that notion I was reminded that part of the significance of Wordsworth's inscription of places as sources of revelation lies in what Geoffrey Hartman calls "the continuum of the wisdom of the dead and the energy of the living."[1] In other words, the spirit of the place is animated by a reverence for the past that is forever mitigated by the present. Therefore to meditate attentively on the Faculty Room is to summon the essence of both—the wisdom of the dead and the energy of the living. For it is the Faculty Room that illustrates this continuum best. The portraits lining the walls reveal its history, and the uses to which the room is put (faculty meetings, tours, trustee meetings, ceremonies) manifest its current vitality. It is the Faculty Room that furnishes me with an opportunity to think of Princeton as not one, but two orders of continuum: the personal and the public. Princeton, for those who have experienced it, is a place of private memory that colors and organizes their everyday life, and a place of collective public memory which has helped to shape the nation's life.

17

Figure 1. Faculty Room, southeast corner.

In the first instance Princeton is a subjective experience of the place itself. It is remembering the trees down Witherspoon Street reaching across the pavement and the shops and the pedestrians to touch each other. Beneath their heads, the street lights are shy and so, if one happens to be there in spring twilight, falling petals descend on the pedestrians and the road like snowflakes in December.

In the second instance Princeton is a place fixed in public memory as part of the history of the nation. Take, for example, another street. Once it was the King's Highway; then it was named after William III, Prince of Orange, of the House of Orange-Nassau; now it is a modern avenue of commerce. Yet once, even longer ago, it was the trail of indigenous Americans, the Lenni-Lenape.

In private memory this place is its halls, its library, its chapel all worn to satin by the encounters and collaborations among and between strangers from other neighborhoods and strangers from other lands. It is friendships secured or lost on greens, in classrooms, offices, eating clubs, residences. It is stimulating rivalries negotiated in laboratories, lecture halls, sports arenas. It is lively discourse debated among faculty in the Room named for its scholars. Every doorway, tree, and turn is haunted by peals of laughter, murmurs of loyalty and doubt, tears of pleasure, sorrow, triumph.

Yet woven into these instances of private memory are others that are the property of public memory: the FitzRandolph Gate locked for years and unlocked for many more; ivy constantly trimmed to reveal and commemorate the ravages of a Revolutionary war; the policy duels of presidents, statesmen, captains of mighty industries.

Portraits in the Faculty Room are those history has chosen to remember. And although the room does not (cannot) accommodate portraits of countless others who facilitated the careers and achievements of the enshrined, and does not represent the contributions of the many who followed in their wake, make no mistake, this place is redolent with the breath of the emotional life lived here and the intellectual life made manifest here where "the wisdom of the dead and the energy of the living" join to become a tradition that informs the present and will shape the future.

When in 1862 President Lincoln told Congress that the "dogmas of the quiet past are inadequate to the stormy present," he was referring to a Civil War waged to suture the wide cut, the open wound, of an already sundered Union. And when he followed that observation with "We cannot escape history," the connotation of the term, history, summoned the future.[2]

Lincoln was alluding to history's future judgment on how and whether the nation could separate dogma from its own past and regard history as events in progress. The founders of Princeton who preceded Lincoln's remarks by 116 years knew well, better perhaps than the founders of any American institution of high learning of the time, the necessity of being open to the unforeseeable. For as Woodrow Wilson said over a hundred years ago, these founders "had no more vision of what was to come upon the country than their fellow colonists."[3] But it was clear that they were determined to enter history—not as into a sepulcher but as into a torrent of contemporary affairs. They were determined to make a place where views different from the authoritarian synod, views considered radical, apostate at the time, would prepare young men for whatever might be asked of them in the service of their God, their conscience, and their province.

Princeton was the place of the independent idea; the place where conscience was prized above orthodoxy; the place of the dissenting idea. Not dissent for its own sake, dissent as style, as fashion, as self-aggrandizement, but dissent over what was fundamental, complex, and urgent to the health of the citizenry—the thrust of an individual's spiritual and intellectual life, the belief that inner experience counted for more than the accepted doctrines of the church. In the 1740s that was indeed a risky proposition. Some believed it an arrogant one, and they may have been right. But if so, it was the arrogance of a sublime idea, not a pedantic one; of a generous idea, not a self-satisfying one.

It is hard now to imagine how fresh were the terms in which those men spoke of spiritual life, of their God; how intense the political debates they held, the metaphysical arguments they advanced; the enemies they must have infuriated, the envy they surely roused. To put forward, without established support, a position so unpopular among educators must have seemed reckless indeed. Yet it was that very independence that helped make Princeton "a national place before there was a nation."[4]

Dissidence and honest disagreement—the marks of lively, new democratic discourse—lurk in the portraits on display in the Faculty Room. *Aaron Burr Sr.* and his predecessor, *Jonathan Dickinson*, now hang side by side (fig. 1; *Burr* at lower left, *Dickinson* to the right), but it was Burr who moved the college from Newark to the village of Princeton, a choice that re-enforced its independence, its insistence upon making its own way. Although, or perhaps because, the place was far from meddling distraction, it was an environment ideally suited to forging the affairs of a new nation. The serene and determined faces of *Jonathan Edwards*

Figure 2. *Jonathan Edwards* (1703–1758), President (1758); 1860. Henry Augustus Loop (1831–1895). After Joseph Badger (1708–1765), ca. 1750. Oil on canvas. Gift of great-grandsons of Jonathan Edwards.

Figure 3. *John Witherspoon* (1723–1794), President (1768–94). Artist unknown; after Charles Willson Peale (1741–1827). Oil on canvas. Gift of friends of the University.

(fig. 2) and *John Witherspoon* (fig. 3) both veil and convey the fierce dissent from orthodoxy that took place in this place. How can we not take pride in knowing that within these walls the first meeting of the state legislature of New Jersey was held, as well as the ceremonial functions of the Continental Congress of 1783? This site bears witness to the stamina, the prescience of the originating idea taking root in hospitable soil.

As a writer and a scholar, I have a personal interest in the translation of tradition, of history, into a livable present and a civilized future. I have personal interests in methods by which histories are disrupted, how intervention can extinguish cultural memory or drive it underground to avoid eclipse. Thus the more than 250-year trajectory of this "experiment" in higher education has great significance for me. I am intrigued by the ways in which an independent idea plays out over time; how it is preserved or altered; and how the place of its birth is both conserved and made new. There are in this country parallel histories of the same nativity, with the same agenda of freedom and dissent, with other landscapes struggling for preservation and for rebirth.

Universities play a powerful mnemonic role. Their fields are dotted with figures, plaques of bronze, stone, and marble, and with botanical life to keep memory alive. But they are not memorabilia or mausoleums. What may suggest stasis in the gender and racial monopoly on display in the Faculty Room will eventually be eclipsed by the inevitable inclusion of President Shirley Tilghman's presence as well as future luminaries not exclusively white or male. It seems clear that the Faculty Room is not a tomb. It is a womb. So while Princeton remains legitimately enthralled with the place of the idea, it must continue to be equally faithful to the idea of the place.

The idea of the place is visionary, is change; it throbs with life, leans toward the edge. The idea of the place is to burrow into the heart of a theory, of a concept; to cast one's gaze toward the limitlessness of the universe; not merely to anticipate the future but, in certain instances, to drive it. The idea of the place despises those forces in academic institutions so fearful of independent thought and alarmed by challenge that they prefer to court irrelevance; institutions so atremble at the tides of change that they are content to rest on past laurels rather than shoulder the hard responsibilities of transformation.

The place of the idea represents the value of tradition, of independence; the idea of the place is its insightful grasp of the future. Negotiating those two ideas, conservation and change, is no small matter. It demands work and intelligence of the highest order. Conservation and change are not necessarily adversarial ideas, and even when they appear so, that irreconcilability is the clash that stirs inquiry and fosters knowledge. The Faculty Room, ringed with the visual presences of George Washington, James McCosh, and Woodrow Wilson, embodies their reconciliation—the place of the idea becomes the idea of the place. There are few territories left, other than universities, where both the wisdom of the dead coupled with the doubt of the living are vigorously encouraged, welcomed, become the very stuff of education, the pulse of teaching, the engine of research, the consequence of learning. No faculty member worth the profession has ever taken for granted as fixed truth or fiat all he or she has learned. The nature of our profession is to doubt, to expand, enhance, to review, to interrogate. But no faculty member is able to question in a vacuum, or is fired up to innovate, to create because she is interested in erasing the inheritance, the authority of her discipline. No student is expected to be satisfied with the acquisition of data, of information.

It is demanded of her or him to move beyond the plateau of what is known to what is knowable, toward more and other knowledge, knowledge that might one day contribute to the wisdom of the past. Tradition is not there to bedevil us. It is there for us. It is not there to arrest us; it is there to arouse us. That is the continuum; that is the reconcilability of tradition and the future.

Because this volume comes upon the heels of anniversaries marking 250 years of Princeton's, and, a decade later, Nassau Hall's existence, monumental milestones which bracket the dawn of a new millennium, it is appropriate to have millennial thoughts. What will Princeton be in 2246, at its quincentennial celebration? By then it will have seen 250 years of the third millennium. What new portraits will grace the Faculty Room? What form will the idea of the place have taken then? Will service to the nation be narrowed to holding public office and wielding private power? Will the entitled still be worried about entitlements? Will gates again be locked? Will the mission have stumbled because the constituency has changed? Will instruction be executed solely in solitude by the isolated handling of sophisticated new machines? Will departments and intellectuals have closed themselves off from the great and tumultuous issues of that future day? Will those hired to guide students to meet those challenges recoil from the difficulty and recreate instead the moribund world of their nostalgia? Will chests swell at the success of having preserved the place and the idea in amber? Will that generation of educators be telling students that not only was everything better before they were born, but that everything before their birth will always be better; that the best they can hope for their future is to clone a former generation's past?

Or will Princeton continue to do what it has done so brilliantly, so often in the past century and a half: revel in the fact that its taproot was fed by the waters of civil dissent, and has been nurtured by sound learning and respect for heterogeneous discourses on the dominant philosophical views of the world. The evidence of the first decade of the twenty-first century, based on the initiatives launched, the symposia held, the arts on display, is convincing. Princeton at its quincentennial will still follow its principal and noblest dictates and continue to wage war for the liberation of power, not just its transfer. It will continue to do what has made it legend and unique among the nation's great universities: remain steadfast in its insistence that a premiere liberal arts education requires students and faculty to face each other in what Woodrow Wilson described as "personal conference and intimate counsel."[5] The evidence of these recent years and under current leadership is unassailable: no priorities will go unmet in enabling this institution to make as constructive a difference in the larger community as it does in the lives of each and every student, regardless of that student's resources; in assuring the best physical environment for staff, faculty, and students; in assembling the best scholars and artists in the world; in enhancing its global influence.

On the other hand, if Princeton University had abandoned the principles upon which the College of New Jersey was founded, then whoever contemplates this historical institution at its quincentennial, will be musing on a "virtual" university—a package of attitudes and preferences emanating from souvenirs, images, and longing, where complacent leadership proved not only unsuitable for the education of the nation's children; it proved dangerous to them. "Those societies which cannot combine reverence to their symbols with freedom of revision, must ultimately decay either from anarchy, or from the slow atrophy of a life stifled by useless shadows."[6] The essays in this volume are testimony to how well Princeton has understood Alfred North Whitehead's warning.

Princeton's subtlety lies in its tradition of independence. Princeton's poise rests on its ability to revise itself. Its strength is knowing what its founders knew, that service to the individual, to the government, to the world requires unwavering commitment to intellectual freedom, to virtues already being debased by apathy or mindless rage: integrity, honor, faith, selflessness, and courage.

In the years to come, between now and the nearly 250 years that will pass before the quincentennial that I am imagining, the world may become overwhelmed by fear and mediocrity, by xenophobia and mendacity. Then universities alone may very well be the last preserve of free thought, of independent inquiry, of simple caring for. Princeton's proud past is that it was the first of such havens. Its bright future is that it will always be. And the walls of the Faculty Room will continue to record for posterity its brilliant balance of conservation and change, tradition and progress.

This volume is a celebration of and re-dedication to: This place. This idea.

NOTES

This essay originated as the convocation address delivered at Princeton University's 250th anniversary celebrations on October 26, 1996, and has been revised for inclusion in this volume to consider the role and significance of the Faculty Room.

1. Geoffrey H. Hartman, *The Unremarkable Wordsworth* (Minneapolis: University of Minnesota Press, 1987), 42.

2. Lincoln's remarks were made at the conclusion of his "Annual Message to Congress," December 1, 1862. See *The Collected Works of Abraham Lincoln*, ed. Roy P. Basler (New Brunswick, N.J.: Rutgers University Press, 1953), vol. 5, 537.

3. From Wilson's landmark address, "Princeton in the Nation's Service," delivered October 21, 1896. See *The Papers of Woodrow Wilson*, ed. Arthur S. Link (Princeton: Princeton University Press, 1971), vol. 10, 12.

4. Don Oberdorfer, *Princeton University: The First 250 Years* (Princeton: Princeton University Press, 1995), 11.

5. Wilson's phrase refers to the preceptorial system he instituted in 1905. See "President Wilson's Annual Report," *Princeton Alumni Weekly*, vol. 6, no. 14 (1906): 252.

6. Alfred North Whitehead, *Symbolism: Its Meaning and Effect* (1927; rpt. New York: Fordham University Press, 1985), 88.

NASSAU HALL

Sean Wilentz

In June 1956, Edmund Wilson, Class of 1916, returned to Princeton University to receive an honorary degree, in conjunction with the fortieth anniversary of his class's graduation and the bicentennial of Nassau Hall. The occasion was slightly awkward. Wilson had great affection for his old college, and especially for the memory of his departed teachers Norman Kemp Smith and Christian Gauss. A few years earlier, when presiding over a set of the prestigious Princeton seminars named in Gauss's honor—and presenting work that would eventually wind up as part of his monumental study, *Patriotic Gore*, edited by another Princeton graduate, Sheldon Meyer—Wilson one day took his friend Leon Edel on a private tour of his former stomping grounds, enthusiastically showing off the architectural highlights. But Wilson had never partaken of the rah-rah bonhomie for which Princeton graduates were, and are, so famous. And more than a few Princetonians regarded Wilson—the bookish, oft-married ex-radical—as a disloyal old duck.

Wilson and his latest (and last) wife, Elena, sensed the underlying tension. The day before the big event, from their guest quarters, they could hear the nearby banging of the carpenters who were erecting the ceremonial graduation stage and dais outside Nassau Hall. "Come and look, dear," Mrs. Wilson remarked (or words to that effect). "They're building your scaffold."

Of course, Princeton did not hang Wilson, even metaphorically, but honored him. And so, outside Nassau Hall, tension gave way to paradox. Wilson was never shy about showing his disdain for the American academy and for what he regarded as its obscurantist obsessions. He did teach now and again, to help make ends meet (though his monotone lecturing style turned off his audiences in droves). Otherwise, he said, "writers are much better off outside colleges." And yet, there he stood, the supposedly defiant freelance man of letters, happily picking up another Princeton degree in front of the most storied academic building in the United States, two hundred years after its completion.

It was not the first ironic moment, nor would it be the last, in the long and eventful history of Nassau Hall.

To walk past Nassau Hall, as I do two or three times each workday, gives only the slightest hints of that history. With its massive brown stone outer walls, the place appears to have been there forever. Dominating the University's Front Campus, it looks, to any well-traveled academic, like the quintessential college administrative headquarters: imposing, serene, and official. (Even the bronze tigers that guard the main entrance are at ease.) Apart from small knots of tourists being led around campus by one of the University tour guides, no one ever seems to enter or exit Nassau Hall. The life of campus is elsewhere, around the classrooms and dormitories, where gaggles of undergraduates, women and men, are perpetually in motion: Nassau Hall is more like a machine that quietly goes of itself. The building is certainly important, especially to a Princeton faculty member, as the place where big decisions are made. But in its tranquil self-assurance, it betrays, at a glance, little of its turbulent—and sometimes paradoxical—past.

While it was still under construction, the place came perilously close to being named Belcher Hall. In 1747, Jonathan Belcher, a devout Massachusetts Congregationalist, was chosen royal governor of New Jersey, and he immediately made a pet project of supporting the fledgling College of New Jersey, then located in Elizabeth. Belcher was shocked at the degraded spiritual condition of Harvard and Yale—where, he said, he had reason to believe that "Arminianism, Arianism and even Socinianism, in destruction of the doctrines of free grace are daily propagated"—and he saw the New Jersey seminary as a potential bulwark of the Lord. Seven years later, when work began on the college's new building in Princeton, the trustees tried to honor the governor for his support by naming it after him. ("And when your Excellency is translated into a house not made with hands, eternal in the Heavens," the trustees entreated him, "let Belcher Hall proclaim your beneficent acts.") Belcher graciously declined, and suggested instead the name Nassau Hall, dedicated to "the immortal memory of the glorious King William III, who was a branch of the illustrious house of Nassau." Thus, thanks to Belcher's modesty, began the tradition that in later decades would lead to the composing of "Old Nassau"—imagine a school song entitled "Old Belcher"—as well as to the adoption of orange and black as Princeton's official colors.

The village of Princeton had been chosen as the college's new home in part because of its proximity to New Light Calvinist Pennsylvania, Delaware, and Maryland, and in part because of its salubrious location on a high ridge, well protected from the then-fearsome New Jersey mosquito. For the new college building, the trustees wanted the finest and most

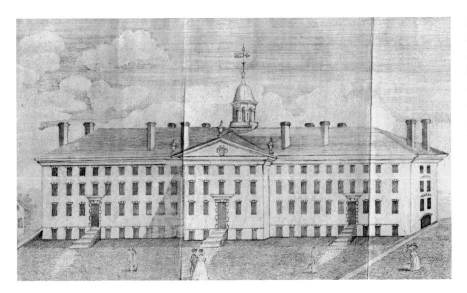

imposing design they could find. A basic plan, offered by the trustee Edward Shippen in 1753, called for a structure 190 feet long and 50 feet deep. Thereafter, Shippen's brother, Dr. William Shippen, in collaboration with the distinguished Philadelphia architect Robert Smith (who had designed Carpenter's Hall, later the meeting place of the First Continental Congress), translated the rough plan into a formal proposal. The cornerstone was laid on September 17, 1754, and for nearly two years workmen raised the walls of local stone and then plastered the interior. In November 1756, as the finishing touches were still being applied, the College of New Jersey officially moved in, claiming an edifice that, though fourteen feet shorter then Edward Shippen's original outline had dictated, still impressed the trustees as "the most spacious on the continent" (fig. 1).[1]

A huge, stylistically up-to-date, Georgian pitched-roof building, the original Nassau Hall was gracious as well as spacious, more so than its later remodeled versions. In contrast to the Old World universities, wrote the college's president Aaron Burr Sr., "[w]e do everything in the plainest . . . manner, . . . having no superfluous ornaments." A depiction of the head of Homer did dominate the flat arch above the building's central doorway, and some decorative urns appeared on the central façade, but otherwise the building had a remarkable lightness for all its solidity, topped off by a bell-tower cupola patterned after the upper part of the cupola of the recently built St. Mary-le-Strand in London, much better proportioned than the current structure.

Figure 2. *A Northwest Prospect of Nassau Hall*, 1807. Jonathan Fisher (1768–1847); after engraving by Henry Dawkins (active 1753–1786), ca. 1764; after drawing by William Tennent. Oil on canvas. Department of Rare Books and Special Collections, Princeton University Library.

Befitting the college's primary function as a trainer of clergy, the original Nassau Hall was a place of devotion as well as of instruction. After entering the central doorway, one passed into a hallway that led straight to the prayer hall, flanked on either side by classrooms. Here, in the unheated north end of what is now the Faculty Room, students would be summoned up by the cupola bell at the crack of dawn for morning worship—an exercise (especially during winter) of bone-chilling piety that did not sit well with later, more secular generations of undergraduates. Below, in the basement, were the kitchen, dining room, and steward's quarters. On the second floor, in a single room, was the library, above which were two rooms probably used for recitations. The building's wings consisted of small suites, most of which included a bedroom and two tiny studies. In 1762, an increase in student enrollment necessitated the completion of student chambers in the basement—gloomy, damp rooms that housed the unluckiest of the first-year pupils.

Like an Anglo-American cloister, the early Nassau Hall almost completely enclosed college life. Here, the college's tutors as well as its students slept, ate, prayed, and attended class. (Only the college president was permitted separate quarters, in a Philadelphia Georgian dwelling, also designed by Robert Smith [fig. 2, at right]).[2] Yet no sooner was the all-encompassing edifice completed than bad fortune descended on the college.

30

In February 1757, President Burr had to step in to fulfill the duties of one of the college's tutors, the Reverend Caleb Smith, who had fallen ill. Six months later, Burr, worn out from overwork, presided extemporaneously at Smith's funeral; then, after a taxing trip to Philadelphia, Burr rode north to Elizabeth to preach a funeral sermon for the suddenly departed Governor Belcher. Finally, himself overtaken by a raging fever, Burr weakened and died on September 24. Five days later, the trustees named Burr's eminent father-in-law, the renowned Massachusetts evangelist and theologian Jonathan Edwards, as Burr's successor.

In January 1758, Edwards arrived at the President's house to great acclaim from the tutors and students. Unfortunately, smallpox was prevalent in Princeton that year, and Edwards, who had never been exposed, decided to submit to an inoculation from the same Dr. William Shippen who had had a hand in designing Nassau Hall. The inoculation did not take, and on March 22, the great Edwards died. His successor, Samuel Davies, was young, eloquent, and learned—but he had also, for years, suffered from tuberculosis, a condition the trustees apparently overlooked. After punishing himself with a dawn-to-midnight work schedule, the dedicated President Davies died after a little more than a year's service. For the third time in the five years since relocating to Princeton, the college solemnly buried its president in the old cemetery down the road from Nassau Hall.

Here, seemingly, was providence ill enough to chill any Calvinist's soul. Supposedly wholesome Princeton had become a president's graveyard. Davies's death, one correspondent reported, "spread a gloom all over the country" and plunged the college into despair.

It was only under the leadership of the eminent Scots émigré and eventual American patriot John Witherspoon, who served as president from 1768 until 1794, that the College of New Jersey truly began to flourish. Witherspoon steadied the institution's finances, increased its endowment, and ventilated its curriculum with the bracing ideas of the Scottish Enlightenment. Before Witherspoon's arrival, the college's scientific equipage was sorely lacking, especially in comparison to Harvard (which boasted numerous stuffed birds and animals, and the skull of an Indian warrior, among other curiosities); but beginning with the purchase of the famed astronomer David Rittenhouse's intricate orrery (a sort of miniature planetarium, installed in Nassau Hall in 1771), Witherspoon quickly closed the gap. Under Witherspoon, the college also generated a hot republican spirit, carried forth into the American Revolution by, among others, three illustrious members of the Class of 1771: Hugh Henry Brackenridge,

Figure 3. *Surrender of Nassau Hall*. Edward Percy Moran (1862–1935). Currently unlocated.

Philip Freneau, and, most auspiciously, James Madison. Witherspoon himself signed the Declaration of Independence in 1776. Under Witherspoon, Nassau Hall even served temporarily, in 1783, as the new nation's capitol. Yet it was also under Witherspoon (and because of the Revolution) that Nassau Hall suffered the first succession of devastating physical blows. And for several years, immediately after the Declaration of Independence, it seemed that the new nation's good fortune was the college's bad fortune—and vice versa.

On December 7, 1776, British forces, fresh from their victories over General Washington's troops in New York, occupied Princeton and commenced what one eyewitness called the "twenty days tyranny." Redcoats pillaged and burned the town's great houses, and suspected rebels wound up imprisoned inside an abandoned Nassau Hall, where a regiment of regulars had taken up quarters, ravaged the library, and turned the basement into a horse stable. Even worse was yet to come. Washington's men rallied on the other side of the Delaware River, and on January 3, 1777, after an all-night march from Trenton, they inflicted their famous disastrous defeat on the British about a mile outside Princeton village. Some of the fleeing British regulars took refuge in Nassau Hall, knocked out windows, and prepared to counterattack—but Washington's artillery hit the building with such lethal force that the British were forced to surrender. (Gouges caused by the cannonade can still be seen on the building's south exterior wall.) Toward the end of the fighting, a rebel cannonball flew through one of the prayer hall windows and smashed the college's portrait of King George II—the signal, legend has it, that led the redcoats to lay down their arms (fig. 3).

Though returned to patriot hands, Princeton was a wreck. ("You would think it had been desolated with the plague and an earthquake," Benjamin Rush observed; "the college and church are heaps of ruins, all the inhabitants have been plundered.") And for Nassau Hall, Washington's victory proved a prelude for further depredations. American soldiers took up residence and stayed for five months, turning benches and doors into firewood, stripping the walls of plaster, destroying the college organ, and covering the floors with what one report politely called "an accumulation . . . of filth." Rittenhouse's orrery, which the British had carefully preserved along with the rest of the college's scientific instruments, became a plaything for the idle Americans and wound up so severely damaged that it could not be fully repaired.[3] When the troops departed in October 1777, doctors converted Nassau Hall into a military hospital where, for over a year, ill and wounded men tried to recover amid the squalid debris.

Slowly—and, in view of what had happened, miraculously—the college also recovered. President Witherspoon, who served in the Continental Congress in Philadelphia from 1776 until 1782, returned to Princeton as often as he could, and with the assistance of one tutor and one professor of mathematics, he oversaw the resumption of classes in nearby private homes during the summer of 1777. Witherspoon also handed Congress a bill for the damage inflicted on college property, and by the end of 1779, he had actually managed to collect nearly twenty thousand dollars in Continental currency. Yet by the time the money arrived, it had so depreciated in value that it could barely cover the cost of patching Nassau Hall's roof, replacing the broken windows, and making stopgap repairs to the classrooms and student living quarters. In May 1782, a newly enrolled student remarked that, inside and out, the building remained badly scarred by the war, with two of its four floors "a heap of ruins."

Local spirits revived in 1783, at a perilous moment for the republic. Menaced by a massed body of mutinous, unpaid Continental soldiers, Congress fled Philadelphia and, at the instigation of their president, Elias Boudinot (a College of New Jersey trustee), the members reconvened in Nassau Hall's barely restored library room. During the war, the British had twice forced Congress to leave Philadelphia; but now, two years after the British surrender at Yorktown and with a peace treaty in negotiations, internal discord sent the representatives packing. For four months (until Congress relocated yet again to Annapolis,

Maryland), the New Jersey crossroads village and its battered college served as the capital of the United States—an embarrassment that made it difficult to gather a quorum of seven states, let alone the nine states required by the Articles of Confederation to ratify a treaty.

Despite the immense difficulties, for representatives and townsmen alike, the interlude greatly improved Princeton's morale. Once they had settled in, the temporary congressional residents found the place suitable, even attractive. ("With respect to situation, convenience & pleasure, I do not know a more agreeable spot in America," Charles Thompson, the Congress's secretary, wrote to his wife, Hannah.) And tutors, students, and townsmen got to share in the excitement of a rousing official Fourth of July celebration, the arrival of George Washington in August for a two-month stay, and, at the end of October, the receipt of the exultant report that the Treaty of Paris had, at last, been signed. "The face of things inconceivably altered," the young student Ashbel Green later commented, amid "the passing and rattling of wagons, coaches, and chairs, the crying about of pine apples, oranges, lemons and every luxurious article." After attending the college's September commencement ceremony, General Washington presented the trustees with a personal donation of fifty guineas. The trustees, much encouraged, duly commissioned Charles Willson Peale to paint a portrait of Washington, which hung for more than two centuries in the Faculty Room before being removed to the University's art museum for safekeeping, still surrounded by the same frame that had contained the battle-destroyed picture of George II.

Congress proved much less grateful than Washington and repeatedly rejected Witherspoon's requests for additional appropriations to restore Nassau Hall. In a preview of Princeton strategies to come, Witherspoon instead turned to graduates and friends of the college for support. He raised more than seventeen hundred pounds, a respectable sum considering the hard times (though, once again, currency depreciation sharply curtailed the collected money's actual value by the time it arrived in Princeton). With the return of fee-paying pupils, along with occasional gifts from graduates, Witherspoon was able to lay aside enough cash to commence rebuilding in earnest. In 1794, the year Witherspoon died, the French traveler Moreau de Saint-Mery remarked that the college's courtyard looked "dirty and unkempt," and that the enclosure wall was in "a deplorable state." Still, the third floor of Nassau Hall had been restored, its roof completely replaced, and its floors and windows repaired. Inside the students' chambers there were new bedsteads and tables, and the hall's interior walls, partitions, and stairways were all thoroughly reclaimed. In 1800, student enrollment climbed above one hundred, and the trustees had to refurbish the basement rooms in Nassau Hall's perennially wet west wing in order to accommodate "the expected additions." There was even talk of enlarging the faculty with new endowed professorships and of erecting additional buildings. "Every sign pointed to a continued rapid growth," noted the University's later official historian, T.J. Wertenbaker. Then, disaster struck again.

At one o'clock in the afternoon on March 6, 1802, as students were filing into Nassau Hall for their midday meal, a fire broke out in the belfry. A senior named George Strawbridge rushed upstairs and unsuccessfully tried to quench the blaze with a pitcher of water, while other students and teachers grabbed what books, furniture, clothing, and personal effects they could carry away. By evening, all but a hundred of the college library's three thousand volumes had been destroyed, and Nassau Hall stood a blackened hulk. President Witherspoon's successor, the devout Samuel Stanhope Smith, had no doubt that one or more members of the college's small knot of freethinking Jacobinical pupils had been responsible. ("This is the progress of vice and irreligion," Smith exclaimed as the fire was spreading.) In fact, a neglectful chimney sweep appears to have been at fault. But the trustees, goaded by Smith, summarily suspended a group of "undesirable characters" suspected of foul play.[4]

Smith's judgment was just as swift—and much less questionable—about rebuilding Nassau Hall. While the students lived and attended class in local homes and boardinghouses, Smith left the supervision of the college to subordinates and spent more than a year canvassing wealthy graduates for contributions to a rebuilding fund. His efforts, along with those of several trustees, quickly raised considerable cash, and the college commissioned the estimable Philadelphia architect Benjamin Latrobe to commence reconstruction plans. Latrobe made some minor alterations, enlarging the cupola, installing new pediments over the three front doors, and paving the hallway floors with brick. (Unfortunately, Latrobe's major contribution, a new iron roof, proved so leaky that it had to be replaced completely.) But because the building's massive original walls had survived the destruction, Latrobe decided against completely overhauling the place in his preferred Classical Revival style, and Nassau Hall retained its essentially Georgian character (fig. 4). The fund-raising efforts, meanwhile, proved bounteous enough to break ground for two entirely new structures—the Philosophical Building (on the site of the present Chancellor Green Library), which housed the college kitchen, dining hall, recitation rooms, and the observatory, and the still-extant

Figure 4. *College of Princeton, New Jersey*, 1837. John Henry Bufford (1810–1870). Lithograph. Graphic Arts Division, Department of Rare Books and Special Collections, Princeton University Library.

Stanhope Hall, set aside for study halls, a new college library, and rooms for the college's two literary societies.

A student rebellion five years after the disastrous fire caused temporary damage to Nassau Hall and lasting damage to the college. In March 1807, three students were suspended, one for getting drunk in a local tavern, one for cursing and insulting a tutor, and one for insulting Professor of Chemistry John Maclean, frequenting taverns, and "bringing strong liquor into the college." Convinced that the suspensions were based on partial and prejudiced evidence, the accused students' friends organized a petition drive, which wound up leading to the suspension of 125 additional students—roughly three-fourths of the entire student body. The same night that the penalties were announced, the discharged pupils ransacked Nassau Hall, warding off alarmed tutors and townsmen with bludgeons fashioned from the building's banisters.

President Smith immediately canceled the classes that remained before the five-week spring vacation, and in due course, with peace restored, fifty-five of the rebels were readmitted.

(One of those who was not, Abel P. Upshur of Virginia, went on to become secretary of state under President John Tyler, only to get blown to pieces in 1844 when a cannon on a great ship he was inspecting—eerily, the USS *Princeton*—unexpectedly exploded). "We will probably have fewer students," one trustee wrote in the aftermath of the riot, "but a few under discipline is better than a mob without any." The first part of this prediction proved true—by 1812, the student body had shrunk to fewer than one hundred, down from the nearly two hundred students enrolled in 1806-7—but the result was penury and stagnation. Pious families feared Nassau Hall was too licentious for their offspring; others feared it was too draconian; and college receipts rapidly dwindled. Thereafter, the college entered nearly two decades of institutional and intellectual decline, a period that Wertenbaker described as "Princeton's nadir."

The turning point—arguably the most important moment in the college's early institutional history—came in 1826, when a group of loyal graduates organized the Alumni Association of Nassau Hall. After electing the aging James Madison as their president, the members dedicated themselves to promoting the interests of the college—including expanding its endowment—and scheduled annual campus reunions at commencement time. The formation of the association was to have a lasting impact on the sum and substance of Princeton life, giving the alumni an unusually close connection to the college's continuing development and originating the annual reunion celebrations that, over the years, have become spectacles of great iconographic (and even anthropological) interest to observers of elite American mores (fig. 5). More immediately, the association raised the money needed for Princeton's first great period of physical and intellectual expansion, including the hiring of new distinguished faculty to endowed professorships (none more celebrated than Joseph Henry, professor of natural philosophy) and, in time, the erection of two new dormitories, dubbed, respectively, East College and West College.

Nassau Hall (which gained the nickname North College) was dingy and drafty compared to the newly built dorms, but into the 1850s, it kept its reputation as the "swell" residence on campus. Aside from the somewhat larger cupola, it would have seemed little changed to anyone who had seen the original as constructed a century earlier. But in March 1855, yet another fire, this one starting in a student's room on the second floor, reduced the place once again to nothing more than its exterior walls. President John Maclean Jr., in office for less than a year, following his predecessor Smith's example, turned to the alumni for rebuilding

Figure 5. Reunion of the Class of 1885, ca. 1900. Historical Photograph Collection, University Archives, Department of Rare Books and Special Collections, Princeton University Library.

funds, and looked to Philadelphia for an architect. Unfortunately, Princeton's choice, the fashionable designer John Notman, was far less circumspect than Latrobe had been, and he initiated an architectural vandalizing of Nassau Hall more damaging than anything the redcoats and rebels of 1777 or the hothead students of 1807 could have imagined.

Notman was a champion of the Florentine Italianate Revival style, first made popular by Queen Victoria's Osborne House on the Isle of Wight and imitated thereafter, in the 1850s and 1860s, by mansion owners and church builders all across England and the United States. Notman himself had brought the style to Princeton with his design for the Prospect mansion on the old Morgan estate near the college (later the president's house, and

Figure 6. *View of Nassau Hall, Princeton, N.J.*, 1860. Robertson, Seibert & Shearman. Chromolithograph. Graphic Arts Division, Department of Rare Books and Special Collections, Princeton University Library.

currently the University's faculty and staff club), and when given the commission to remodel Nassau Hall, he tried his best to turn the old Georgian pile into a squat squared-off, arch-windowed imitation Tuscan villa. He was restrained by the college's demand that he utilize the surviving original walls; otherwise, though, he let his imagination run wild. The old central doorway was replaced by an arched stone entrance, above which Notman built a stone balcony with a large arched window. At either end of the building, he added square Italianate towers, both of them rising a full story's height above the roofline. Atop the entire building he placed a new cupola, much larger than its predecessors, that utterly dominated the building beneath it (fig. 6).

Notman also changed the building's interior. The old staircases flanking the central entrance were replaced by winding red-stone steps in the new towers. Partitions arose across the east and west hallways in order to discourage student pranksters and rioters; new hallways connected adjacent rooms to create single rooms; a new library room was placed on the building's south side; and the entire place was joisted with galvanized iron as a fireproofing precaution. The improvements, especially in the spacious new library, were obvious, and when workmen hung Peale's portrait of Washington (which had been rescued yet again from the flames) on the library's north wall, a clear connection was made with the old Nassau Hall. But when students finally returned in August 1856, they occupied a very different structure from the one completed exactly one hundred years earlier.

Nassau Hall's second century, from John Notman's restoration to the awarding of Edmund Wilson's honorary degree, was much less turbulent than the first—and, architecturally, much kinder. During the decades after the Civil War, the building of additional dormitories led to the departure of the resident undergraduates, replaced first by museums and laboratories and, after the completion of Palmer Laboratory and Guyot Hall in 1909, by academic administrators. (John Grier Hibben, president from 1912 until 1932, was the first president to have his office in Nassau Hall, and beginning in 1924, the building was devoted completely to offices of the University's central administration.) Notman's most egregious error, the brooding Italianate towers at the building's eastern and western ends, was partially corrected in 1905, when the tops of the towers were cut down to conform with the main building's roofline. (Notman's grandiose cupola had been earlier improved by the installation of a four-faced neo-Georgian clock in 1876, a donation from the Class of 1866 in honor of their tenth reunion.)

The outstanding positive contribution of the 1856 restoration, the new college library, was rendered superfluous when the nearby Chancellor Green Library was completed in 1873. After serving for more than thirty years as the college museum, the room was handed over in 1906 to architect Raleigh Gildersleeve, who designed the impressive Faculty Room. Modeled on the British House of Commons, the room is still used for faculty meetings, debates, and official convocations. Thirteen years later, in the patriotic aftermath of World War I, the firm of Day and Klauder redesigned the building's entrance hall as a marble memorial to Princeton's war dead, beginning with the names of ten former students killed in the American Revolution (fig. 7).

Figure 7. Nassau Hall War Memorial. Cushing–Gellatly (photographers). Historical Photograph Collection, University Archives, Department of Rare Books and Special Collections, Princeton University Library.

Figure 8. Class of 1896 Ivy. Historical Photograph Collection, University Archives, Department of Rare Books and Special Collections, Princeton University Library.

41

Figure 9. 1879 Tigers cartoon.
John M. Foster (Class of 1917).
Princeton Tiger Magazine (1915).

Tom—These are the famous '79 Tigers.
Ethel—Where are the other 77?

Decorative elements also sprouted up outside Nassau Hall, at odds with President Burr's old admonition against "superfluous ornaments," but not with the building's basic integrity. Beginning sometime in the 1860s or 1870s, successive groups of graduating seniors planted ivy around the building's wall, marked off by discrete inscribed stone tablets (fig. 8).[5] In 1879, the graduating seniors—including one Thomas Woodrow Wilson—presented a pair of sculpted lions (adapted from the House of Nassau's crest) to guard the hall's entryway (see fig. 5). Thirty-two years later, when the lions were much the worse for wear—and by which time, worse still, the tiger and not the lion had become Princeton's mascot—the same class donated the two recumbent, placid bronze tigers, designed by the renowned sculptor A.P. Proctor, that continue to adorn the main entryway (fig. 9).

A year after Proctor's tigers appeared, President Hibben was inaugurated—and the young Edmund Wilson arrived for his freshman year. A generation later, when Wilson received his honorary degree, Nassau Hall was virtually unchanged. And so, apart from some interior and minor exterior alterations finished in 1967, Nassau Hall remains the same today.[6]

Time has softened most of the old wounds, including the self-inflicted ones. Not that the old spirit of unrest has completely departed. By moving the administration's nerve center to Nassau Hall, the University (so renamed in 1896) ensured that, from time to time, Nassau Hall would be a staging ground for protests, by activist students (most notably over the war in Vietnam in the 1960s [fig. 10] and over Princeton's investments in South Africa fifteen years later) and, more decorously, by complaining faculty members (over the entire panoply of University issues).

Still, the prevailing note today is of sturdiness and tranquility. It takes some historical research, and a little historical imagination, to see beyond all that to a deeper appreciation of what the building has been through, and what it stands for. No longer the largest structure in town, dwarfed by the towers of Gothic dormitories and postwar science labs, Nassau Hall is, on close inspection, far more than an administration building: it is a battle-scarred monument to the University's—and the nation's—continuities and changes. As I pass by and see it, artificially illuminated, at workday's end, it glows as an emblem of Princeton's better nature, which is to be (as Woodrow Wilson proclaimed in 1896) a university "in the nation's service."

Inside the truncated unfortunate Italianate towers, countless footfalls have worn down the stone steps into venerable slopes, blending in with the genuine Georgian surroundings.

Figure 10. Nassau Hall student protest, ca. 1970. Historical Photograph Collection, University Archives, Department of Rare Books and Special Collections, Princeton University Library.

And, from a distance, even Notman's cupola looks more graceful with the passing of years, vaulting above the small forest of Front Campus, breaking through the modern car-infested clamor of Nassau and Witherspoon streets, beckoning to what Edmund Wilson called the "languid amenities" of a place of great privilege and great learning.

NOTES

This essay has been adapted from one originally featured in *American Places: Encounters with History*, edited by William E. Leuchtenburg (Copyright © 2000 by Oxford University Press, Inc.) and appears here with the kind permission of Oxford University Press.

1. It was, in fact, the largest stone building, and the largest academic building, in the colonies.
2. The house still stands. Known today as Maclean House, after the mid-nineteenth-century president John Maclean Jr., it contains the offices of the University's Alumni Council.
3. Exhibited at the World's Columbian Exposition in Chicago in 1893, the orrery disappeared until it was discovered, still in its packing crate, in the basement of McCosh Hall in 1948. Thanks to the generosity of Bernard Peyton, Class of 1917, the contraption was then fully restored, though with a modern electric motor. The restored orrery is on permanent display in the lobby of Peyton Hall.
4. It is unclear from the surviving records whether five or six students were suspended.
5. The oldest tablet reads "1870," although University records state that ivy was planted at the gymnasium that year. The first reference to any ivy planting occurs in 1864, though where on campus this took place is unclear. The graduating Class of 1865 planted woodbine at Nassau Hall. My thanks to Ann Halliday and John S. Weeren for this information.
6. The 1967 renovations involved flooring over the two-story well in the east wing to provide additional office space, as well as the removal of an unsightly skylight above the east wing. See Alexander Leitch, *A Princeton Companion* (Princeton: Princeton University Press, 1978), 331.

MEMORY AND MEANING IN THE FACULTY ROOM

KARL KUSSEROW

Notable among the transactions at the December 18, 1849, meeting of the board of trustees of the College of New Jersey—or Princeton College, as it already was known—is an item resolving "that the Vice-President be requested to take measures to collect as many of the Portraits of the Officers and Trustees of the College, as can be obtained." In authorizing such an initiative, the century-old institution endorsed the creation of a durable and potent means of self-representation and signaled its continued vigor following periods of instability, stagnation, and outright decline. The trustees' directive further specified that the assembled portraits be placed "in the Portrait Gallery," the largest room in the college's Nassau Hall nexus, which had until then served as a prayer hall. The dedication of this central space away from the Deity to focus instead on the institution's household deities was meaningful, as was the shift in function more generally, anticipating a succession of diverse uses to which the room was put over time, each of them reflecting the evolving concerns of the college and the wider world it inhabited.[1]

This essay tells that story—the narrative of two intertwined histories, of the portraits and of the space at the heart of the institution that brought them into being—and in the process explores the broader implications of both, not just within but also beyond the walls of Nassau Hall. What ultimately emerged in 1906 as today's Faculty Room is a place devoted, through the pictures it contains, to the historical representation of Princeton University, and it boasts a "biography" as compelling as those of the individuals displayed throughout the room. Few American spaces hold such history. Prayer hall, battle scene, government seat, portrait gallery, library, museum: the Faculty Room's varied past encompasses significant moments in early national history while more expansively reflecting, over the long arc of its existence, fundamental institutional—and wider social and cultural—transformations in epistemic emphasis, from a world essentially knowable through recourse to God, to one increasingly oriented around the humanistic traditions represented by libraries and museums,

to one, finally, in which the history of certain American institutions, like Princeton, become venerable enough to provide and sustain their own internal logic.

But before any of this transpired, Nassau Hall and its prayer hall stood for years in a field atop a rise in the small town of Princeton. It is hard now to imagine the effect the building—enormous by contemporary standards—must have had, looming up from the meadow, dwarfing its sparse wooden neighbors. Photography wasn't invented until nearly a century after its construction, so there is little to help conjure the scene, though a vintage photograph from around 1870 showing the cupola of Nassau Hall and the college's several buildings begins to suggest it (fig. 1). What emerges from the picture is a sense of the school's isolation, before the town grew up around it, and, somehow, despite the buildings' heft, of its fragility, all the more so in the increasingly turbulent world of eighteenth-century America. Few of the several dozen students clustered then in the prayer hall for services could have envisioned either the future of that space or the institution it would come to embody.

In the Beginning

In the beginning, at the College of New Jersey, there was indeed the Word, and it was proclaimed, early and often, in the prayer hall. The first academic exercise held in Nassau Hall, on November 13, 1756, was a prayer service. Every day thereafter, for the near-century of the room's use for that purpose, students and faculty gathered before dawn and again in the evening to avow their devotion according to the evangelical Presbyterianism that ushered the college into existence. The prayer hall gave material expression to the school's pronounced religiosity. Although much has been made of Princeton's early accommodation of both religious and secular education, were it not for the need to train Presbyterian ministers to propagate the beliefs of the fervent "New Sides"—adherents, unlike their conservative "Old Side" counterparts, of the First Great Awakening—Nassau Hall would never have been built. While the oft-quoted phrase of one of the school's founders expresses the hope that it would prepare men to be "Ornaments of the State as well as the Church," that same statement begins with the affirmation that "our great Intention was to erect a seminary for educating Ministers of the Gospel." Shortly before his appointment as Princeton's first president, Jonathan Dickinson (fig. 2) similarly wrote, "Our Aim in the Undertaking is to promote the Interests of the Redeemors Kingdom; and to raise up qualified Persons for the sacred Service."[2]

Yet in also "encouraging and promoting a learned Education . . . wherein Youth may be instructed in the learned Languages, and in the Liberal Arts and Sciences," as the college's second charter reads (the first, politically tenuous document of 1746 having been superseded two years later by a more viable one), the intent was clearly not just to create a school for the production of divines. Like Yale a half-century before it, the college was founded out of dissatisfaction with the paucity of and perceived lack of piety among existing educational options for ministerial, as well as for lay, purposes. Whereas the ten Congregationalist ministers who instituted the Collegiate School (as Yale was first known) were reacting against the alleged doctrinal laxity of Harvard, where each of them had been trained, the seven original founders of the College of New Jersey—all but one, Yale alumni—were in turn motivated by a desire to fashion an institution more closely in accord with their intense religious zeal. In so doing, they drew upon influences that included Princeton's academic predecessors in Massachusetts and especially Connecticut, but also the nonconformist tradition of England's dissenting academies and, more locally, the short-lived Presbyterian seminary known as the Log College in Warminster, Pennsylvania, from which the school drew many of its early leaders.[3]

Figure 2. *Jonathan Dickinson* (1688–1747), Founder, President (1747). Edward Ludlow Mooney (1813–1887). Oil on canvas. Gift of the artist.

A sense of Princeton's initial priorities comes across visually in the earliest surviving image of its Nassau Hall home, an illustration that appeared in the March 1760 issue of *The New American Magazine* (fig. 3). Depicting a structure still recognizable in its rudiments today, the engraving shows Nassau Hall set upon a bare and unpopulated plain, with the same air of isolation as in the photograph taken a century later. Yet a countervailing impression of comforting order and solidity also emerges from the carefully rendered parallel lines out of which the building takes shape, an effect enhanced by the pair of cherubs holding aloft a banner bearing the college's motto, "Dei Sub Numine Viget" (under God's power she flourishes). Centered directly above the cupola of Nassau Hall, the motto prescriptively, and rather hopefully, trumpets the explicit causal link between the Deity and the new institution's progress and fortitude. Also pictured above Nassau Hall, but off in a corner, boxed and contained in its

Figure 3. Nassau Hall, from *The New American Magazine*, March 1760. Henry Dawkins (active 1753–1786). Nassau Hall Iconography, University Archives, Department of Rare Books and Special Collections, Princeton University Library.

own mediating frame, is a vignette displaying the tools of earthly knowledge—microscope, dividers, telescope, sextant, globe, and books—illuminated through the clouds by the sun's strong rays. The relationship between the vignette, with its artifacts of secular humanism, and the banner, tying the college's future to divine sovereignty, is a telling expression of the artist's impression of the young college. The only two compositional embellishments of the otherwise matter-of-fact illustration, they suggest that while there is room in the picture for the emerging light of reason, in the world Princeton College was constructing, God held center stage.[4]

A similar centrality distinguished the prayer hall, located at the back of the building behind the projecting pediment visible in the engraving, and seemingly as austere as the landscape shown surrounding it. "We do everything in the plainest & cheapest manner, as far as is consistent with Decency & Convenience, having no superfluous Ornaments," President Aaron Burr Sr. (fig. 4), who had moved the college into its new home, informed a correspondent. He was speaking

Figure 4. *Aaron Burr Sr.* (1716–1757), Founder, President (1748–57). Edward Ludlow Mooney (1813–1887). Oil on canvas. Presented by John Maclean.

generally of Nassau Hall, which despite its status as among the largest buildings in the colonies was built to be more sturdy than deluxe. Clergyman Ezra Stiles, the future president of Yale, "[v]iewed the foundation & plan of college at Princetown" on October 1, 1754, as construction began, and traced the hall's dimensions in a sketch, later lost but recorded as showing a space thirty-six feet in width and perhaps forty feet deep, including a fifteen-foot projection from the rear of the building. Apparently fascinated by the structure, thirty years later he sketched it again, providing the earliest known plan of the building's footprint (fig. 5), one subsequently codified and elaborated in the volume produced to celebrate Nassau Hall's bicentennial (fig. 6).[5]

Though generally unembellished, the new building was sufficient that "good order is kept in it, [and] useful learning, together with the great doctrines of the Reformation, & the power of piety are successfully promoted," as founding trustee Gilbert Tennent (fig. 7) wrote the year following its completion. One can imagine him ardently reprising from the

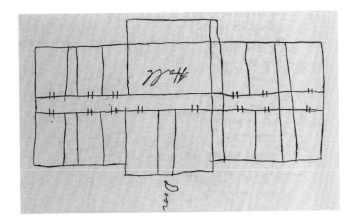

Figure 5. Sketch of Nassau Hall from the diary of Ezra Stiles, September 1784 (image inverted to correspond with plan below).

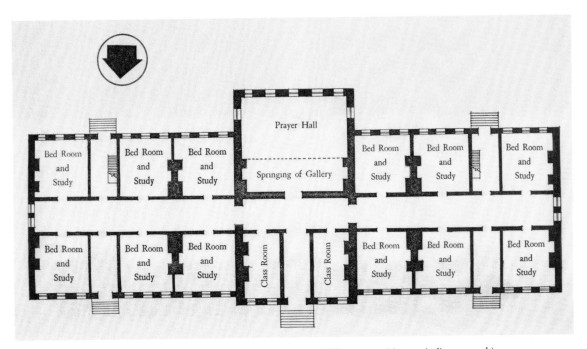

Figure 6. Nassau Hall plan, from Henry Lyttleton Savage, *Nassau Hall: 1756–1956* (arrow indicates north).

rostrum in the prayer hall his most famous sermon, "On the Danger of an Unconverted Ministry," a castigation of clergy not in line with the Great Awakening's quickening energies. Some evidence exists that a certain effort was made to furnish the prayer hall beyond the "plainest & cheapest manner" of the rest of the building. The Reverend Samuel Blair's

Figure 7. *Gilbert Tennent* (1703–1764), Founder, Trustee (1747–64). Jacob Eichholtz (1776–1842). Oil on canvas. Gift of Miss Smith.

Figure 8. *Ashbel Green* (1762–1848), Class of 1783, President (1812–22). Artist unknown. Oil on canvas. Gift of Mr. Stockton Green.

enthusiasm in promoting the fledgling institution probably caused him to exaggerate when describing "an elegant hall, of genteel workmanship . . . with a neatly finished front gallery," but if extra attention was devoted to any part of Nassau Hall, it would have been to the space dedicated to worship. In a later address to alumni, Princeton's eighth president, Ashbel Green, Class of 1783 (fig. 8), recalled the layout of the double-height space during Colonial times, describing a "pulpit," or rostrum, on the eastern wall, accessed from a raised gallery along the northern end, and an organ on the western side, of which "only the frame remained, while I was a student."[6]

From the beginning there were portraits enlivening the hall. The first depicted Governor Jonathan Belcher, who had facilitated a second charter when the validity of the first was attacked by unsympathetic Anglicans. A Congregationalist, Belcher referred to the college as his "adopted daughter"; such was the appreciation of the trustees for the governor's sustained advocacy that they proposed naming the school after him—thus affording subsequent Princeton historians the opportunity to remark on posterity's gratitude for his modesty in declining the honor. Among Belcher's many benefactions to the college, which included his valuable library, was "[m]y picture at full length," installed, as befitted a grand patron, opposite the rostrum on the western wall of the prayer hall. It was joined in January 1761 by a regal representation of King George II (although it did not arrive until several weeks after the monarch's death). No sooner had the king's portrait been hung across the hall from the likeness of Belcher than it inspired a reference in Trustee Reverend Blair's eulogy of January 14 on the late king, lamenting "that thine Image should yet attract our Eyes, if its more admired Original be obscured in Death!"[7]

Blair's encomium notwithstanding, it is interesting to consider the distinction between the two portraits facing off in the prayer hall. While the pictures of the powerful pair each communicated a message of sanction and legitimacy, displaying an image of the local Protestant Belcher was far more in keeping with the college's ideals than one of the distant Hanoverian king, whose Anglicanism and limited grasp of English would only have enhanced the sense of disjunction students must have felt when glimpsing his likeness behind the speaker on the rostrum, railing against the very religion the monarch embodied. Indeed, it is likely George II never knew about either of the charters establishing the institution that had been granted in his name, in part because supporters of the college feared arousing dissent among its Anglican detractors.[8]

Whatever discomfiture the contraposed portraits may have caused did not last long. Sixteen years after the arrival of the royal portrait, both paintings were destroyed during the Battle of Princeton (fig. 9), on January 3, 1777, when American forces under George Washington defeated British troops in and around Nassau Hall, where the English had been garrisoned. The engagement came on the heels of a substantial Christmas Day victory at Trenton, consolidating morale and providing crucial momentum after a series of disheartening defeats. In a well-attested twist of fate, as the battle raged, a cannonball from an American battery—possibly commanded by a young Alexander Hamilton—sailed through a prayer hall window and into the portrait of George II. The portrait of "the late King of Great Britain," as the trustees minutes recorded the event six years later, "was torn away by a ball from the American artillery in the Battle of Princeton." Better still, Ashbel Green later recalled, "There is testimony which is accredited, that the shot took off the king's head."[9]

Figure 9. *The Battle of Princeton*, ca. 1782. James Peale (1749–1831). Oil on canvas. Gift of Dean Mathey, Class of 1912.

Nassau Hall itself fared little better. Prior to the battle, it had served for a month as British barracks, storehouse, and, in the stone cellar below, dungeon—and during the conflict, control over it changed hands fully three times. The English were likely to have been especially hard on the building throughout their occupancy, knowing it to be a bastion of the despised Presbyterians, who constituted more than half the Continental Army and whose ministers were seen as fomenting the Revolution. Moreover, the college was led by the Scot John Witherspoon (fig. 10) who, as a signer of the Declaration of Independence and member of the Continental Congress, had been a particularly strong supporter of independence. (Speaking of Witherspoon in Parliament, antiquarian and wit Horace Walpole observed that "cousin America had run off with a Presbyterian parson.") After the battle, American troops were no kinder, though the depredations of their five-month tenancy—including harvesting the prayer hall's pews, rostrum, and the pillars of the gallery for firewood—must have been motivated more by necessity than ideology. In any case, the combined effect of the damage incurred before, during, and after the Battle of Princeton led diarist Ebenezer Hazard to conclude, "The College is in a very ruinous situation. . . . [E]very room in it looks like a stable."[10]

Nor had much changed by the summer of 1783, when none other than the government of the United States took up residency in Nassau Hall. Following the departure of American soldiers, Witherspoon attempted to repair the building, and in September 1779 was able to reconvene the college there after holding classes in local homes. But progress was slow. Ashbel Green, not yet a student but residing nearby, reported that "the dilapidation and pollution of the college edifice, when left by its military occupants, extended to every part of it." Nonetheless, during this period the prayer hall continued to be used, "both for the students and the people of the town, who worshipped together," as Green also recorded, in this way anticipating the far grander public service to which the space was put from late June through

Figure 10. *John Witherspoon* (1723–1794), President (1768–94). Artist unknown; after Charles Willson Peale (1741–1827). Oil on canvas. Gift of friends of the University.

Figure 11. *Elias Boudinot* (1740–1821), Trustee (1772–1821). Artist unknown. Oil on canvas. Anonymous gift.

November 1783. The Congress of the Confederation, as the American government was formally known, was eager to escape Philadelphia that summer, after a mutinous group of Maryland soldiers (who feared being discharged without back pay following the cessation of hostilities) had surrounded the legislators in the Pennsylvania State House for three tense hours on June 20. When the Pennsylvania militia did nothing to intervene, Princeton resident and college trustee Elias Boudinot (fig. 11), then presiding over Congress, offered Nassau Hall as a temporary alternative. The delegates readily agreed, and quickly established themselves there, probably using the upstairs library for routine affairs and reserving the prayer hall for larger and more ceremonial events—in part out of necessity, as there was little left in the room to accommodate them. It must have been an extraordinary few months, with members of Congress jostling up against faculty and the fifty-odd students in the cramped quarters of the building, whose ruined condition and explicit vestiges of battle were clear reminders of all that had brought them there. Yet it was a fitting place for Congress to convene, given the school's uniquely strong contribution to both the prosecution of the war and the institution of the new government it had enabled. An astonishing ninety-seven percent of Princeton's graduates are known to have sided with the patriots when war began; eighty-eight held positions of responsibility in the American military, and alumni later constituted a disproportionately high number of congressional and other government representatives. It made still more sense that Congress met formally in the prayer hall, for the leaders of the college, like many of the delegates, were united in the belief that success in the fight for independence must ultimately be accorded to Divine Providence.[11]

By all accounts the culmination of that remarkable summer—which included the reception in the prayer hall of Washington himself, greeted by a seated Boudinot, signifying the transfer of military to civilian power—related not to Congress but to the college. At the September 24 commencement exercises, Washington and delegates of Congress, among them seven signers of the Declaration of Independence and two future U.S. presidents, heard a future Princeton president, the same Ashbel Green, deliver an impressive valedictory address so praising of the general it caused him to blush. Witherspoon offered a prayer, an oration in Latin was pronounced, and members of the Whig and Clio debating societies disputed moral and political questions. The graduation ball lasted until dawn. Following the serious matters of state transacted over the previous three months, the celebratory high spirits of commencement must have been a relief and a hopeful portent to the assembled leaders, who recognized in the graduating class—as in the college itself—a group imbued with the same combination of Christian, republican, and Enlightenment ideals that informed the new nation. As for the prayer hall, its use as the theater for such diverse affairs of school and state foreshadowed the eventual devotion of the space, decades later, to secular concerns. Indeed, while prayers were still held there twice daily, and though the circumstances that caused the room to serve as national headquarters were extraordinary, under Witherspoon the college underwent a subtle but unmistakable shift toward secularization, evident in both curricular changes and career choices of graduates, which themselves reflected broader societal transformations.[12]

Meanwhile, at the meeting of the trustees held the day after that memorable commencement, the college's leaders, "being desirous to give some testimony of their high respect for the character of his Excellency General Washington," and wishing to honor the hero's presence in their midst, appointed "a committee to wait upon his Excellency to request him to sit for his picture to be taken by Mr. Charles Willson Peale of Philadelphia." Flattered—or perhaps feeling indebted to them for the gesture—the next day Washington

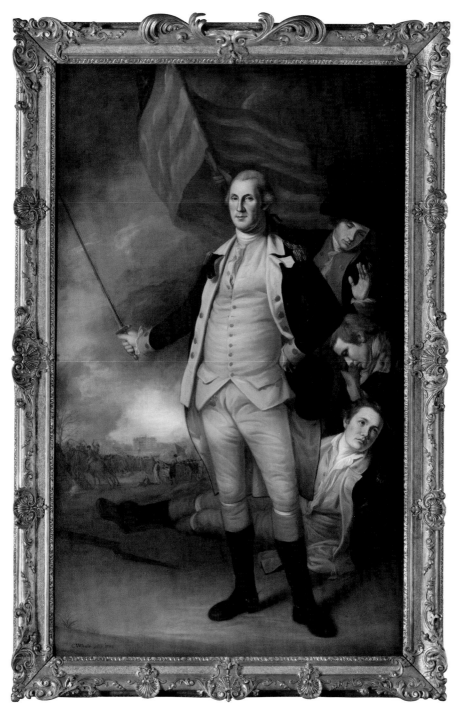

Figure 12. *George Washington at the Battle of Princeton*, 1784. Charles Willson Peale (1741–1827). Oil on canvas. Princeton University, commissioned by the Trustees.

returned the favor, and Witherspoon duly reported that the general had "delivered to him fifty guineas which he begged the trustees to accept as a testimony of his respect for the college." The honored sitter having thus effectively paid for the portrait himself, the painting was ordered, and in December 1783, Washington granted Peale the fifth of his unsurpassed seven sittings with the future president. The resulting portrait, *George Washington at the Battle of Princeton* (fig. 12), was completed by the following commencement, and probably installed in the prayer hall in person by Peale, who on October 19, 1784, wrote, "I painted a picture of Genl. Washington for Prince Town Collidge and was at the Commencement, much Entertained."[13]

Peale's selection for the commission was particularly apt, as he had actually participated in the Battle of Princeton as a company leader in the Philadelphia militia. It is not known whether the college dictated the precise terms of the picture's appearance, but it must have been expected that the artist would produce an image of the decisive local engagement in which he had served, in which the college had been heavily implicated, and during which Washington had especially distinguished himself for bravery. What seems certain is that Peale was requested to make a portrait sized to fit the frame of the decapitated *George II*, which had more lately housed the coat of arms of the sympathetic Governor Belcher. While the desire to reuse the elegant British frame for the new portrait of Washington was probably motivated as much by its rare quality as by an appreciation of the inherent irony of the switch, this act of Revolutionary recycling added another symbolic layer to the frame's history.[14]

Peale had in fact already painted another version of Washington at Princeton for the Supreme Executive Council of Pennsylvania, and several replicas after it—one of which was eventually donated to the University (as the college had by then become known). Entitled *George Washington after the Battle of Princeton* (fig. 13), that painting shows the general at ease in the aftermath of the battle, leaning proprietarily on the muzzle of a cannon, as if to underscore the conflict's end and successful outcome, while in the background captured redcoats are regimented away from their Nassau Hall redoubt. More artifacts of stagecraft than history painting, the replicas were disseminated to royal palaces abroad as diplomatic tools to bolster the new nation's legitimacy. For the college, by contrast, Peale produced a unique composition, whose distinctions are suggested by the different prepositions their titles employ. *Washington at the Battle of Princeton* conjures the battle itself, and makes specific reference to

Figure 13. *George Washington after the Battle of Princeton*, 1779–82. Charles Willson Peale (1741–1827). Oil on canvas. Bequest of Charles A. Munn, Class of 1881.

events from it, notably the death of Washington's friend General Hugh Mercer, shown expiring in the arms of surgeon (and Princeton alumnus) Benjamin Rush (fig. 14), a blood-stained bayonet nearby indicating the cause of death. Above them, Washington, his sword poised in readiness, gestures toward the raging battle, where Continental troops, pistols and muskets blazing, force British soldiers away from Nassau Hall—or, in the pictorial logic of

Figure 14. *Benjamin Rush* (1746–1813), Class of 1760; 1823. John Tickell Viner (active 1818–1854); after Charles-Balthazar-Julien Fevret de Saint-Memin (1770–1852). Oil on canvas. Gift of John S. Pierson, Class of 1840.

the painting, literally off the picture place and out of existence, in the direction Washington's raised weapon appears to impel them. Meanwhile, a diminutive horseman bearing a white flag, just visibly rendered approaching from Nassau Hall (fig. 15), makes apparent that Mercer's ultimate sacrifice was not in vain. (In Charles Willson Peale's brother James's rendition of the battle [fig. 9], which he also experienced firsthand, the fallen Mercer can be seen in the background being tended to by a fellow soldier [fig. 16].)[15]

The more detailed historical character of Peale's painting for Princeton, and the comparatively formal pose Washington takes in it, made sense for this particular commission. The artist would have known the picture was intended to replace a similarly official state portrait of George II, and he must have intuited the appeal to his patron of featuring Nassau Hall's role in the conflict, and, more subtly, of portraying Washington as if in protection of it. In any case, the commission was both a grand and an appropriate gesture for the battle-scarred institution. Peale's painting suggested Princeton's continued vitality (a role portraiture was to serve again for the college) while manifesting its allegiance to the nation's revolutionary ideals. There is a remarkable symbolic narrative to the displacement of the portrait of

Figure 15. Detail of *George Washington at the Battle of Princeton* (fig. 12).

Figure 16. Detail of *The Battle of Princeton* (fig. 9).

George II, which in 1777 occupied the prayer hall much as the British occupied the land surrounding it, with the portrait of another George, who led the Battle of Princeton that destroyed the first painting, and whose image not only supplanted—in the very same frame—that of the monarch, but did so in a depiction of the actual victorious event. Whether or not such subtleties were recognized by contemporary viewers, the special nature of the painting did not go unnoticed. On a visit to Princeton in 1787, Reverend Manassah Cutler of Connecticut remarked, "The Hall is ornamented with several paintings particularly the famous battle in the town." Few American paintings, and, indeed, few portraits anywhere, are so elaborately involved in their own history.[16]

Trial by Fire

The Reverend Cutler's reference to the "several paintings" in the prayer hall must remain unclear, as no documentation of them exists, and certainly the pictures themselves do not. They perished along with much else in Nassau Hall in the disastrous fire of March 6, 1802, which left most of the building a black and gutted shell. While the Washington portrait was saved, little else remained, and President Samuel Stanhope Smith (fig. 17), perhaps seeking an earthly explanation for what the humbled trustees termed "the frown of Divine Providence," concluded that "circumstances strongly lead to the belief that the fire was communicated by design" of certain students hostile "to religion and moral order." Having promptly suspended them, Smith steadfastly vowed, "The college will be rebuilt and its discipline rendered still more strenuous and exact to meet the spirit of the times." Similarly unbowed, the trustees determined "without the least delay, and with the utmost vigor, to adopt measures for rebuilding the College edifice." To the general effort to reconstitute the institution, President Smith rather hopefully added, "All Specimens of Elegant Execution in the Fine Arts will be thankfully received," though none, apparently, were forthcoming.[17]

True to their resolve, by the end of that summer one of the school's tutors reported that "the edifice is rebuilding with great speed" under the supervision of esteemed Philadelphia architect Benjamin Latrobe. The prayer hall, which since the fire had been sufficiently rehabilitated to also temporarily serve as repository for the few books left to the college, was returned the following spring to its usual sole purpose when they were moved to the new library (now Stanhope Hall), one of two smaller buildings Latrobe had erected with funds left over from the subscription to repair Old Nassau.[18]

Figure 17. *Samuel Stanhope Smith* (1750–1819), Class of 1769, President (1795–1812). Charles B. Lawrence (ca. 1790–1864). Oil on canvas. Gift of friends of the University.

Having overcome its trial by fire, the college was soon again tested, and by the same element Smith had earlier blamed for its physical ruination: unreformed students. The infamous student riot of March 1807, begun in reprisal for the college's punishment of a few classmen for disorderliness but ultimately resulting in the suspension of most of the student body and the closure of the college for weeks, was a blow from which it took the institution far longer to recover. While student unrest was not uncommon on college campuses during the early nineteenth century, at Princeton it hardened a growing opposition to Smith, whose ability to maintain a properly robust Christian orientation in the face of rising scientific and honored republican values (under whose mantle the rioters had defended themselves) came increasingly into question. By 1812 Smith had resigned, the formidable Ashbel Green was installed as Princeton's eighth president, and the school took on a new, more self-consciously pious cast, even as some of the same trustees who engineered Smith's departure instituted the nearby Princeton Theological Seminary to ensure the satisfactory preparation of the Presbyterian ministry.[19]

Following this period of pronounced instability there began a much longer one of decline, from which it seemed the college might never emerge. Many students had not returned to Princeton after the riot, enrollment languished for years, and student disturbances continued among those who did matriculate. Green's decade-long tenure was not without its successes (a religious revival among students in 1815 pleased him greatly), but it also ended with his resignation; the first decades of the century were unsettling times for the College of New Jersey. James Carnahan (fig. 18), like each of his predecessors a Presbyterian minister—but unlike them, initially ill-prepared for leadership—assumed the presidency in 1823 and held it for a record thirty-one years. During the early years of his tenure, the college reached its lowest point, with ongoing student turmoil, a forty percent decline in enrollment (to a mere seventy-one students in 1827), and serious financial shortfalls leading to faculty unrest and resignations. At one point, Carnahan considered recommending closing the school permanently.

Curiously, it was at the height of this sustained malaise that a young and energetic professor, John Maclean, Class of 1816 (fig. 19), began what was to be a lifelong campaign to collect portraits of Princeton's leaders and notables. The son of the college's first professor of chemistry, and himself trained as a minister, mathematician, and linguist (in keeping with the school's broadening focus), Maclean devoted himself throughout his extended Princeton career more to the institution itself—its history, alumni, and traditions—than perhaps anyone before or since. In beginning to do so at its weakest moment, he seems to have recognized the value of history, and historical portraiture, in institutional invigoration. The rhetorical use of the genre to bolster an institution's present through reference to its past has a long history of its own, and Maclean's desire to start collecting portraits when he did sent a message of Princeton's strength and confidence at a time when such associations must have been particularly welcome. Indeed, Maclean's focus on the past, as studies of nostalgia have shown, in part belies still greater concerns about the present, even as it suggests an astute awareness of the iconicizing power of portraiture in representing the college's lengthening history.[20]

As early as 1825 Maclean corresponded with Samuel F. B. Morse (at that time still more artist than inventor) about a commission to paint renowned botanist and physician David Hosack, Class of 1789, who was especially celebrated within the college for attending the

Figure 18. *James Carnahan* (1775–1859), Class of 1800, President (1823–54); 1850. Edward Ludlow Mooney (1813–1887). Oil on canvas. Gift of Mrs. Hannah McDonald.

mortally wounded Alexander Hamilton, LL.D. 1791, following his duel with Aaron Burr Jr., a member of the Class of 1772 and the son of Princeton's second president. That portrait never materialized, but in 1826 another one did. It was painted by Charles Willson Peale's son Rembrandt, who wrote, "I have bestowed as much attention and care as if you had offered me one hundred guineas," suggesting the impoverished school was unable to come up even with Peale's customary fee (which Maclean and Carnahan seem to have paid themselves). "Besides," Peale continued, "the destination of this Portrait is sufficiently flattering to both parties to induce us to make some effort in rendering it valuable to your institution"—a statement expressive of both the college's prestige, despite current conditions, and the merits of portraiture in maintaining it.[21]

Figure 19. *John Maclean* (1800–1886), Class of 1816, President (1854–68); 1850. Edward Ludlow Mooney (1813–1887). Oil on canvas. Gift of President Maclean.

That same year, Maclean made further efforts in institutional advancement by establishing the Alumni Association, through which he sought to raise funds and solidify ties to the college, helping ensure its future much as he hoped portraiture might by materially representing its past. An aged James Madison, Class of 1771 (fig. 20), agreed to serve as president, with the unassuming Maclean becoming secretary, a position he occupied with characteristic endurance for more than half a century. The organization of the alumni was a significant success, yet it was slow going with the portraits, to say the least. It is not precisely known when the next pictures were acquired, but an 1849 letter to the trustees from Maclean—by then vice president of the college—indicates the "collection" amassed during the intervening twenty-four years totaled precisely six portraits. Apart from its disappointing length, the list reveals

Figure 20. *James Madison* (1751–1836), Class of 1771. Jacob Cist (1782–1825); after Gilbert Stuart (1755–1828), 1804. Oil on canvas. Gift of Gilbert S. McClintock, Class of 1908.

that whatever efforts there were had been desultory in nature, as much the result of happenstance as any systematic program. That was soon to come, but in its sluggish and haphazard beginnings, Princeton's modest collection mirrored other contemporary academic assemblages, such as the one at Brown University, the Baptist analogue to Presbyterian Princeton, which received its first portrait in 1815, commissioned its second two decades later, and didn't begin acquiring pictures of institutional worthies in earnest until the 1850s. Still, Maclean followed up his list with the anticipation that "several of the friends of the College have promised to add to this collection by presented portraits of some of the distinguished Trustees and officers of the College now numbered with the dead. A few of these portraits will probably be received in the course of the next session; and when they are received, the whole collection will be placed in the Old Chapel." Hence, just as Maclean was recounting the collection's spotty progress to date, his portrait initiative seemed finally to be coming into its own.[22]

As indeed it was, although without the energetic support of the trustees, who lacked, initially at least, Maclean's keen regard for institutional history and portraiture, and a sense of how the two might work together in Princeton's self-representation. In 1846 the trustees had authorized the construction of a new chapel, but equivocated on the use to which the again-growing college's increasingly cramped prayer hall might be put. Their meeting minutes for June 26, 1847, record that "repairs were in progress" toward "fitting up the Old Chapel for a Portrait Gallery," but by December of that year practicality appears to have trumped portraiture: "Resolved, that the building committee be authorized to have the Old Chapel converted into Rooms for the accommodation of Students." As it happened, however, "The committee on fitting up the Old Chapel with Rooms for Students Reported that nothing had been done, and Recommended that the Chapel be fitted up for a Portrait Gallery, and the report was adopted." With space now to display them, the trustees got on board in promoting portraiture at the college, as the *Princeton Whig* reported at the end of 1850: "The Trustees of this venerable institution are endeavoring to secure a portrait of each of the Presidents of the College, and of the early Governors of the State, as [ex-officio] members of the Board of Trustees, and of the other Trustees, and thus to form a most interesting collection of paintings."[23]

The *Whig*'s announcement indicates not just the college's eventual sanction of the portrait program but also the intent to systematize it through the acquisition of portraits of only a certain type—the school's executive leadership (presidents and trustees), as against, more generally, distinguished faculty, alumni, and friends. In so articulating the scope of the collection, the institution signaled a desire to move beyond the random accumulation of "such portraits and paintings as may come into the possession of the college," as Maclean had put it, and toward a more standardized mode of ordering its representation and history. In this it mirrored its institutional contemporaries, such as the New York Chamber of Commerce, whose collection—eventually perhaps the most impressive among American institutions—began with a similarly circumscribed programmatic focus. The acquisition of a set of leadership portraits provided a means for organizations to visually and materially manifest, and thereby clarify, their often complicated pasts. Princeton's collecting project served a similar impulse to use portraiture to impose structure, sequence, and unity on its own lengthening history. In this way it was like any number of ordering discourses to emerge around 1850, as growing professionalization engendered more refined processes of organization rooted in cataloguing and the development of systems for classification, and as grander, all-encompassing explanatory narratives appeared—the Great Exhibition of 1851, Darwin's *The Origin of Species* in 1859, encyclopedic museums of science and art in Boston in 1870 and New York in 1869 and 1872—to simultaneously contain and elucidate an increasingly complex reality. Princeton's comparatively modest effort to reify its history through portraiture represented its contribution to this overarching trend.[24]

In articulating a genealogy for the college, the portraits further provided a tangible connection to the storied past, linking the institution to the glory of highly esteemed men and to an era often deemed nobler than the present. Americans throughout the country at the time responded to a disconcerting sense of remoteness from the great men and high ideals of the revolutionary era with an array of historical, preservation, and other retrospective projects, of which Princeton's portraits can be seen as a part. Perhaps because of this desire to reconnect with a past thought rapidly disappearing, most institutional portrait collections, including Princeton's, widened and eventually abandoned their narrow focus to embrace instead the whole of their historical constituency. By the 1880s the New York Chamber of Commerce was collecting portraits of not just its presidents but also officers and esteemed members, and Brown seems to have done so from as early as the 1850s.[25]

Neither image nor extensive description of Princeton's original portrait gallery survives. We know from the *Whig* announcement that by 1850 the prayer hall's "stage, pulpit, and gallery ha[d] been removed" to accommodate the space's new use; in their stead, the article continued, "the walls are already graced with the portraits of Presidents Burr, Witherspoon, Smith and Green and of Judges Paterson [fig. 21] and Kirkpatrick and Wm. Stockton and Mr. Lenox, and with Peal's [*sic*] inimitable likeness of General Washington taken in 1783." While the removal of the chapel to its own newly constructed edifice expressed the college's ongoing commitment to its religious roots, the replacement in the central space of pulpit with portraits, many depicting men distinguished for accomplishments of a secular nature, also bespoke the college's widening focus, and that of the world around it. The collection of portraits Maclean began, and the dedication of the room at the heart of the college to contain them, had emerged out of a confluence of personal interest, institutional evolution, and broader cultural trends. With it, Princeton elucidated and honored its past, even as the portraits bolstered its present—and, in their installation in the historic room at the back of Nassau Hall, anticipated their later deployment in that same space as the defining feature of the next century's Faculty Room.

Figure 21. *William Paterson* (1745–1806), Class of 1763, Trustee (1787–1802). Mrs. B.S. Church (dates unknown); after James Sharples (ca. 1751–1811), 1794. Oil on canvas. Bequest of William Paterson, Class of 1835.

Phoenix

The second fire to rage through Nassau Hall, on March 12, 1855, was from the perspective of the portraits far less serious than the first. Although it, too, left the building in ruins, with only the walls standing—"magnificent even in their desolation," as the *New-York Daily Times* described it—unlike in 1802, the portrait collection was saved. The blaze had begun on the second floor and, abetted by spring winds, quickly spread. "At an early period of the fire," the *Times* continued, "even before the building was, by most persons, considered in danger, the door of the picture gallery was forced open by Mr. Cameron, one of the tutors, and Mr. Gilchrist, a member of the senior class. They were soon joined by professors Giger and Duffield, and others, citizens and students, eager to rescue the portrait of Washington by the elder Peale, and the portraits of the earlier Presidents and friends of the College." The dedication of all hands—"citizens and students"—to remove the portraits "without injury to a place of safety," and the consistent mention of their efforts in accounts of the fire, suggest that in the few years since its establishment, the collection had assumed a position of real

significance. By then numbering perhaps two dozen paintings, it was already an institutional touchstone, to be secured even in the face of danger.[26]

The collection's enhanced role in the life of the college is further suggested by the concern for its continued accommodation. As in 1802, and with a confidence born of the school's steadily strengthening circumstances, the trustees immediately determined to rebuild, the *Princeton Press* assuring readers "the friends of old Nassau Hall will not rest until she rises again like a Phoenix from her ashes." From the start, the portraits factored into their plans, which initially called for a separate skylit gallery over the new library envisioned for the space where the prayer hall and the first, short-lived portrait gallery had been. Within two weeks of the fire, John Maclean, appointed Princeton's tenth president in 1854, received from Philadelphia architect John Notman a "plan & elevation" providing for such a gallery, probably at Maclean's suggestion. Eventually gallery and library were combined into a single large space, significantly longer and taller than the prayer hall had been (fig. 22), with room for books as well as portraits. When interior work was complete and the library finally opened in 1860 (the panic of 1857 evidently having slowed fundraising efforts), the trustees' Building Committee proudly described the space: "The Library Room is large, beautifully proportioned, and chastely finished. It is 74 feet in length, 36 feet wide, and 30 feet high,"

Figure 23. Nassau Hall Library interior (from south), 1868. J. Moran. Albumen print. Historical Photograph Collection, University Archives, Department of Rare Books and Special Collections, Princeton University Library.

nearly twice the size of the old prayer hall. Contemporary views show an interior that is indeed chaste, with plenty of room both on the walls and in bookcases for future growth (fig. 23). The committee further specified, "The floor is . . . of slate, supported by iron beams, and arches of brick"—even the shelves were made of stone—underscoring the imperative for the twice-burned space to be as flame-retardant as possible, "that the College may have a room in all respects suitable for its Library, and for its collection of portraits."[27]

Proud as the college was of the enlarged and refurbished space, it wasn't necessarily easy to experience. When Maclean's successor James McCosh (fig. 24) arrived from Scotland by way of Belfast to take up his duties, he found a library "open only once a week and for one hour. This seems strange to me," the learned minister continued, but in fact it was not unusual in American colleges at the time, where books, despite their increasing numbers and decreasing cost, were often regarded as precious icons of knowledge, to be guarded rather than opened. At Harvard, the normally stern scholar and librarian John Langdon Sibley was seen one day crossing the Yard, smiling, because "[a]ll books but two are in, and I am on my way to get them."[28]

But however removed from the daily experience of Princeton students the library may have been, it was clearly a significant place in, moreover, a highly significant space. The

Figure 24. *James McCosh* (1811–1894), President (1868–88); 1886. John White Alexander (1856–1915), Hon. 1902. Oil on canvas. Gift of alumni.

installation there, at the epicenter of the college—by then sufficiently grown to merit the term "campus" that Witherspoon invented for it—of first the portraits, and then the library, materially expressed the institution's ongoing evolution away from its churchly beginnings, and toward the world of men and their books.[29]

Maclean's retirement in 1868 did not end his efforts on behalf of the college and especially its portrait collection. Around that year he made a list of the collection thus far, which though it survives only in fragmentary form, suggests the group had grown to some thirty paintings, most of them gifts of family members memorializing deceased relatives. The list further reveals that the focus remained on the school's leadership, although several long-serving faculty and even a few alumni had also come to populate the assembly. Significantly, portraits were now sometimes paid for by the college itself, which enabled it to more effectively control collecting patterns. A December 1860 report contains notice "[t]hat the Trustees approve the suggestion of the President in regard to procuring a portrait of the late Professor Hope, and that a sum not exceeding $50 be appropriated for that purpose." While such a figure (equivalent to little more than $1000 today) would only have resulted in a portrait of modest size by a painter of similarly modest talents, what mattered was that the trustees were now routinely appropriating funds for portraiture.[30]

McCosh's administration saw both consolidation and growth in the college, which he sought to make "equal to any . . . in America, and, in the end, to any in Europe," as he had confidently announced at his inauguration. The portrait collection grew in step with the school. At some point during his tenure, the set of presidential portraits was completed, such that McCosh could claim it among his accomplishments at the end of his presidency twenty years later. Offering an unbroken visual chain of institutional history and memory, the presidential portraits solidified Princeton's past, constructing it as linear, stable, even dynastic, when in fact it had been punctuated by periods of doubt, inactivity, and decline. In this way, the collection tapped into one of the great strengths of institutional portraiture, which glosses history such that all is and always has been well among groups availing themselves of it. That the school could do so through the trustworthy and reassuring visage of one clergyman after another, with patriots and scholars also thrown in the mix, only heightened the effect. Looking at the serene and kindly portrait of Ashbel Green (fig. 8), it seems hard to imagine that as a young trustee he once surreptitiously investigated the president of the college, his predecessor Samuel Smith (fig. 17), and ultimately helped engineer his removal—only himself to later resign under a cloud. Such is the power of portraiture in re-presenting history.[31]

Implicit in the collecting and display of the college's leadership portraits was the notion that its past might be approached and understood through them and the lives they represented. Indeed, the fulfillment under McCosh of the biographical project the portraits constituted merely reflected the larger reality that the college conceptualized itself and its history more through men than deeds or events. Such an orientation was natural for an institution that prided itself on the character and quality of its leaders, but it also drew upon broader cultural trends. Just as Princeton's collection was getting underway, the June 1845 issue of the *Yale Literary Magazine* asserted, "Biography has obtained . . . a degree of attention and importance

Figure 25. *Jonathan Dickinson Sergeant* (1746–1793), Class of 1762, A.M. 1765; 1786. Charles Willson Peale (1741–1827). Oil on canvas. Gift of Jonathan Dickinson Sergeant III.

it never before enjoyed. . . . [I]n fact, Biography is the rage of the day." This "biographical mania" was an international phenomenon of particular strength and longevity in England, where it helped bring about the National Portrait Gallery in 1856 and was given influential expression by Thomas Carlyle in an 1840 lecture entitled "The Hero as Divinity": "Universal history, the history of what man has accomplished in this world, is at bottom the History of the Great Men, those great ones; the modellers, patterns, and in a wide sense creators, of whatsoever the general mass of men has contrived to do or to attain." At Princeton, the construction of history as biography dovetailed with the institution's just pride in its leaders—whose devout Presbyterian sameness moreover evinced a desirable consistency—to help produce the institution's own portrait gallery, through which its past might be both materialized and celebrated.[32]

Figure 26. *Samuel Davies* (1723–1761),
Hon. A.M. 1753, President (1759–61); 1874.
James Massalon (active 1850–1881). Oil on
canvas. Presented by John Maclean.

The use of portraiture for such nonaesthetic ends helps explain the college's apparent lack of concern for originality or for quality in building its collection, neither of which was the point. This too was typical. When the New York Chamber of Commerce lavishly published its renowned portrait holdings, even it was compelled to begin: "The purpose of this collection has not been so much to gather fine specimens of the art of portraiture in painting or sculpture . . . but to preserve the lineaments of those men who have illustrated the commerce of New-York." Princeton did collect some fine portraits (fig. 25), but also many copies and indifferent originals. Above all, the portraits were placeholders in the institutional story, and the acquisition of any image, whether good or bad, served equally well in its completion. Again and again in the 1850s, 1860s, and 1870s, John Maclean turned especially to his friend, artist Edward Ludlow Mooney, as well as to others, to paint requisite portraits from whatever sources were available—including, for a portrait of President Davies (fig. 26), "a photograph of a print believed to be a likeness" of the long-deceased preacher.[33]

The extent to which the college conceived and conveyed its identity through the collected identities of its "Great Men" was emphatically revealed in its representation at one of the nineteenth century's greatest spectacles, the 1893 World's Columbian Exposition in Chicago. For months in advance of the event, committees of both trustees and faculty

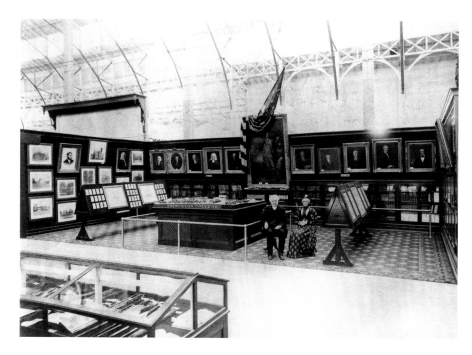

Figure 27. Princeton College exhibit at the World's Columbian Exhibition, Chicago, 1893. University Archives, Department of Rare Books and Special Collections, Princeton University Library.

planned and debated how best to portray the college to the masses of expected visitors. In the end, they decided to focus on the institution's history, a history communicated largely through portraiture. A photograph of McCosh and his wife seated at the Princeton booth (fig. 27) shows walls covered in portraits, with images of the school's leaders flanking the flag-draped *George Washington after the Battle of Princeton*, thereby situating the institution within the context of the nation's wider history. "There is no exhibit which is more pleasing in its general effect," the *Princeton Press* proudly declared; "the historic character of Princeton is made a prominent feature of the exhibit. The south wall contains a row of ten oil paintings of the former presidents of the college." Thus capitalizing on the current vogue for historical portraiture—itself an expression of the broader nostalgia and antimodernism then affecting the fast-changing country—Princeton pictured itself not so much through its present as by way of its past. In so doing, it underscored how central portraiture had become to its self-imagining.[34]

Meanwhile, back in Nassau Hall, the portraits had some time ago been joined by rather unlikely companions (fig. 28). The completion in 1873 of the larger Chancellor Green Library meant the removal of books from the portrait collection's midst; in place of them,

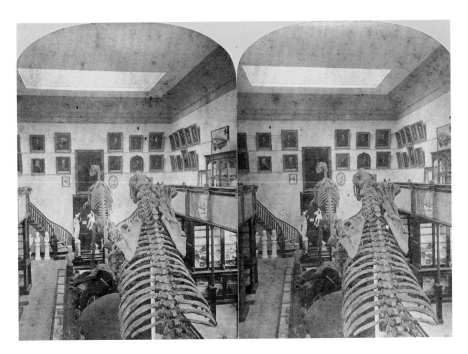

Figure 28. E. M. Museum in Nassau Hall, 1875. Mead & Beard. Stereograph. Historical Photograph Collection, University Archives, Department of Rare Books and Special Collections, Princeton University Library.

McCosh proposed refitting the space as an ambitiously expanded Museum of Geology and Archaeology. It was not the first time the college museum would occupy the former site of its library—that had happened before when the school's books were returned to Nassau Hall and the old library (now Stanhope Hall) was rechristened Geological Hall—but in this instance it signaled the growing importance of science at the college, which McCosh viewed as essential in its transformation into the great university he envisioned. The repurposing of the historic space, now for the fourth time, from chapel to gallery to library to museum, reflected the new prominence of an entity that had been "rather wandering in its character . . . hustled from one room to another," as the *Nassau Literary Magazine* described the old museum, even as it more generally expressed Princeton's evolving character, aims, and concerns. In preparation for the change, a raised gallery was built around the perimeter of the space and a substantial new skylight was installed in the roof. The result, as the *Princetonian* reported, was that "[t]he room seems to be as well fitted for its intended use as one could wish." Renowned geographer Arnold Guyot, a professor since 1855, was charged with the interior design of what by 1875 had officially become the E.M. Museum, after an anonymous benefactor. Explaining the room's layout several years later, he noted, "The first twenty feet of the hall,

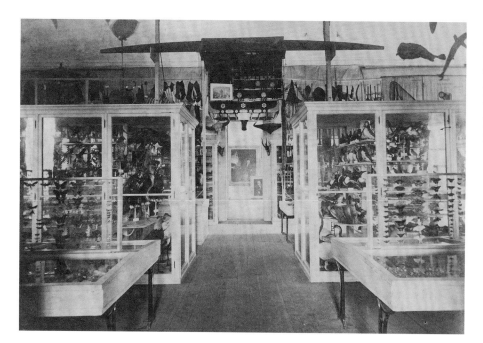

which mark the space occupied by the original College Chapel, are reserved for the collection of memorial portraits of the Presidents, professors, and illustrious friends of the College," suggesting an awareness of the paintings' stature and a desire to maintain their link to the history and heart of Nassau Hall.[35]

The evident rationale underlying Guyot's placement of the portraits reflected a broader logic informing the museum's installation. Despite its jumbled appearance to contemporary eyes, the E.M. Museum was no haphazard Victorian cabinet of curiosities. On the contrary, its scientific collections were considered second only to the Smithsonian's, and were similarly intended both to instruct and to advance the limits of knowledge. In this the museum in turn reflected, while in fact helping to lead, the era's wider museological, scientific, and indeed epistemological evolution toward the increased specialization and classification of knowledge, itself the product of the ever growing data produced by institutions like Princeton newly dedicated to research. The quasi-taxonomic orientation of institutional portraiture fit neatly into this schema, both in Nassau Hall and elsewhere, as at Brown University, whose historical portraits were exhibited beginning in 1874 in Rhode Island Hall alongside artifacts from its Museum of Natural History (fig. 29).[36]

Figure 30. E. M. Museum. Historical Society of Princeton.

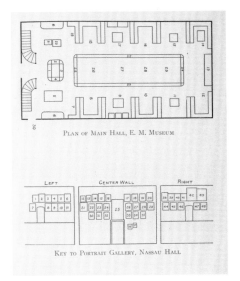

Figure 31. "Plan of Main Hall" and "Key
to Portrait Gallery," from John Rogers
Williams, *Handbook of Princeton* (1905).

Figure 32. *Cretaceous Life of New Jersey*, 1875–77. Benjamin Waterhouse Hawkins (1807–1894). Oil on canvas. Princeton University, Department of Geosciences.

Figure 33. E. M. Museum, ca. 1886. Pach Brothers. Albumen print. Historical Photograph Collection, University Archives, Department of Rare Books and Special Collections, Princeton University Library.

Underscoring the museum's didactic function, Guyot referred to the gallery as his Synoptic Room, where "the leading idea in the arrangement . . . is that [the displays] should strike the eye as an open book in which the student can read, at a glance, the history of the creation from the dawn of life to the appearance of man." The room's diverse geological, paleontological, and archaeological contents were all arrayed to this end. So, too, in their way, were the portraits (fig. 30). Just as the exhibits of physical artifacts were intended to demonstrate the triumphal progression of life (whether directed by God or Darwin's theories was a matter of strenuous contention at the time), so the relics of Princeton's institutional narrative were arranged in a manner rendering it not only coherent and comprehensible, but similarly cogent and inevitable. A key to the portrait gallery (fig. 31) from a later *Handbook of Princeton* diagrams the paintings' "evolutionary" hanging, with the presidential portraits serially displayed along the left and right walls of the raised gallery, allowing close inspection. The guide appears in the handbook just beneath a floor plan providing the broader layout of the museum, the one reinforcing the other in mapping a place characterized by system, order, and a compelling surety.[37]

Another set of paintings also appeared in the room. Explicitly developmental in nature, the seventeen canvases depicting prehistoric life commissioned by Guyot in 1875 from British scientist and natural history artist Benjamin Waterhouse Hawkins supplied the perfect analogue to the portraits. On panels set into the exterior of the gallery balustrade, they presented a progressive pictorial account of life itself, from its imagined invertebrate beginnings through the development of mammals (figs. 32, 33). And if this weren't enough to evoke a sense of progress, the statue of a flying Mercury positioned at the head of the room seemed to urge the whole ensemble forward.[38]

President Wilson's Senate Chamber

James McCosh retired in 1888, having achieved more than perhaps any of his predecessors in the furtherance of the college. His presidency brought Princeton to the brink of the "equal to any" scope and stature boldly envisaged at his inauguration twenty years before. Not only science but the arts now flourished, graduate studies were actively pursued, the number of faculty and students had more than doubled, and the campus stood transformed to accommodate it all. Summing up his achievement in a tribute at the time of his death, six years later, the trustees concluded, "The results of his Presidency have made a new epoch in our history.

Figure 34. *Francis Landey Patton*
(1843–1932), President (1888–1902);
1901–02. John White Alexander
(1856–1915), Hon. 1902. Oil on
canvas.

The College has virtually become a University." Indeed, McCosh had proposed just such a change in name. Although it would have to wait until Princeton's sesquicentennial in 1896, that the term "university" could even be broached was a testament to the transformation he had led. It seems appropriate, then, that the portrait McCosh left behind to commemorate his tenure was also something new (fig. 24), of a different order of both quality and scale than the modest head-and-shoulders portrayals of previous Princeton greats. Painted by John White Alexander, Hon. 1902, while he served as drawing instructor at the college (his very presence on campus made possible by McCosh's broadening influence), the expansive portrait calls attention to itself more as art than mere representation, with an engaging focus on the subject's interior state. Its addition to the portrait gallery lent the collection an increased sophistication, in keeping with the heightened standards of an institution on the rise.[39]

In 1902, Alexander produced another portrait of a Princeton president, McCosh's successor, *Francis Landey Patton* (fig. 34). Patton's portrait was similarly ambitious, though the presidency it memorializes could not approach that of McCosh. Even so, under Patton the school consolidated its gains and continued to grow. That same year, following Patton's resignation (in part the result of dissatisfaction over his less than stellar administrative abilities), Princeton's most renowned president, Woodrow Wilson (fig. 35), assumed office. Though his tenure was to be characterized as much by tumult as by triumph, he inarguably left the school a changed and more substantial place. Wilson had arrived at Princeton from Wesleyan University in 1890, and quickly became prominent among the faculty and beyond as a speaker and writer. At his inauguration, he delivered the aspirational address, "Princeton for the Nation's Service," articulating the rechristened University's enhanced agenda both at the beginning— "[i]n planning for Princeton . . . we are planning for the country"—and at the end of his speech: "A new age is before us, in which, it would seem, we must lead the world." To facilitate its goals, Wilson proposed the introduction of a tutorial system on the British collegiate model, whose intimate nature promoted teacher-student contact and exchange. What emerged in 1905 was the innovative preceptorial system, in which fifty new junior faculty—effectively doubling their number—complemented the lectures of more senior scholars through intensive discussion meetings involving only a few students. Though costly, Wilson's initiative was a success, and aspects of it remain in place at Princeton today.[40]

One effect of the expansion in faculty was the need of a space large enough for them to meet, the old room in the University Offices Building (as the current Stanhope Hall was by then called) having been outgrown for the purpose. As if to signal the University's increased sense of itself, Princeton turned to its most revered space: "The matter of changing the central hall of Nassau Hall into a Senate Chamber was discussed and referred to a committee . . . to report upon the advisability of placing the collections, now in the central hall, in the Old Gymnasium," the trustees recorded in June 1904. A note in the *Princeton Alumni Weekly* the next year confirms that a decision had been made, and as a result, "[i]n the south wing of Old North, where the ancient mastodon has held sway over the ossified birds and beasts of

Figure 35. *Woodrow Wilson* (1856–1924), Class of 1879, University President (1902–10); 1929. Sidney Dickinson (1890–1980). Oil on canvas. Gift of William Church Osborn, Class of 1883, and friends.

the secondary, tertiary, quaternary, etc., ages, and the gigantic reptiles have frightened juvenile visitors time out of mind, a 'Senate Chamber' is under construction." But while the dinosaurs would have to go, the portraits were meant to stay. Indeed, their presence was a significant factor in the "Colonial" design that architect Raleigh Gildersleeve developed for the new meeting space, which from the start he clearly intended to be grand (as his response to an apparent concern of trustee Moses Taylor Pyne would suggest: "[t]he throne can very easily be suppressed"). In particular, English oak wainscoting, lavishly carved, was imported

Figure 36. Faculty Room. J. Moran. Historical Photograph Collection, University Archives, Department of Rare Books and Special Collections, Princeton University Library.

to panel the walls, at a cost far exceeding all other renovations, including the replaced roof. Later, a *Daily Princetonian* article on "The New Faculty Room" explained the rationale behind the expense: "This wood forms an excellent background for portraits, with which the walls are to be covered." Hence the collection was finally to receive its just due, displayed in opulent and sympathetic surroundings in what, the article continued, was expected to be "the finest Council Chamber in the country" (fig. 36).[41]

At the room's opening on November 2, 1906, the exercises began with a prayer, in a nod to the original use of the space, initiated a hundred and fifty years before. Speakers continued to reference its history and venerability, as when trustee and former U.S. President Grover

Figure 37. Harvard University Faculty Room, University Hall, 1936. Harvard University Archives, HUV 39 (9-9).

Cleveland began his remarks: "I almost fear to speak lest I may by some ill selected word or ill considered thought disturb the spell created by the associations of this place." The preserved notes for President Wilson's speech similarly pick up on the theme: "This ground, the historical centre of Princeton's life[,] this Hall the heart of that life. . . . We shall expect to live here always in the presence of the past." In dedicating the hallowed space "to serve a double purpose both as council chamber and picture gallery," as a review of the project in *Architecture* magazine put it, the school explicitly linked its present governance and direction to the sustaining strength of the past and the portraits that embodied it. And by constructing its own institutional Valhalla, filled with the countenances of the school's great leaders, Princeton announced it had fully arrived as a university of note, able to conceptualize itself as a historical entity on its own terms, with a past long and distinguished enough to sustain the narrative.[42]

Figure 38. Sayles Memorial Hall, Brown University, ca. 1881. Brown University Library.

Other American institutions of similar age did the same at the time. In 1896, Harvard completed its own Faculty Room (fig. 37), constructed—just as at Princeton—out of the space formerly occupied by the College Chapel. Brown University's even earlier Sayles Memorial Hall (1881), although not specifically intended for meetings of the faculty, housed the school's chapel and a room displaying portraits of its presidents and leaders (fig. 38), evincing a comparable linkage between institutional lineage and the religious past. Grander still, the always secular New York Chamber of Commerce unveiled its sumptuously cavernous Great Hall in 1902 (fig. 39), at the star-studded opening for which Grover Cleveland also delivered breathless oratory. And plainly following Princeton's lead, Dartmouth College's remarkably similar Faculty Room debuted in 1911 (fig. 40), located as well in the school's main administrative building. What each of these impressive spaces had in common was the use of an

Figure 39. Great Hall, New York Chamber of Commerce Building. New York Chamber of Commerce Collection, New York State Museum, Albany.

institution's past—whether through reference to religious origins, portraiture, architecture, or some combination of each—to legitimate and uphold its present authority.[43]

The shape Princeton's particular expression of this strategy ultimately took was conditioned by factors both internal and external to the University. Gildersleeve's putative Colonial design (in actuality far too ornate for that) was part of a larger effort to "recolonialize" Nassau Hall in the wake of Notman's rather unsympathetic makeover, an initiative more broadly in keeping with the prevailing Colonial Revival style. Wilson himself seems to have been behind the plan to truncate the outsized Italianate towers Notman had tacked on the building's flanks. In the summer of 1905 Gildersleeve sent him "revised elevations of the turrets which show the changes you wished to see." In restoring Nassau Hall and its "old assembly room . . . along the lines of Colonial architecture to something of its original dignity," as the *Architecture* review characterized the renovation, Wilson and Gildersleeve had the crucial support of powerful trustee and benefactor Moses Pyne, for whom Gildersleeve

Figure 40. Dartmouth College Faculty Room, Parkhurst Hall. Rauner Special Collections, Dartmouth College Library.

had recently completed extensive Colonial Revival additions to Drumthwacket, Pyne's elaborate Princeton estate.[44]

But the imported walls of the Faculty Room betokened another, even stronger influence coursing through it, as through campus generally: that of England and its august traditions, academic and otherwise. Both McCosh and the Bermuda native, Patton, were British subjects, Pyne was the son of one, and Wilson and Graduate College Dean Andrew West were confirmed Anglophiles. On trips to England in 1896 and 1899, Wilson visited Oxford and Cambridge, seeing as others had in their architecture a model for Princeton. He wrote his daughter, Jessie, "Oxford, you know, is England's great university town. We hope Princeton will be like it some of these days,—say about two hundred years from now." He wouldn't have to wait that long. Already the turreted Blair Hall (1897) announced the arrival in New Jersey of the architecture of Oxbridge. And so, soon thereafter, and on a smaller scale, would the Faculty Room. If something of the English collegiate dining hall lurks in its

Figure 41. Jesus College Dining Hall, University of Oxford, ca. 1949. F. Frith & Company (postcard).

Figure 42. Worcester College Chapel, University of Oxford, ca. 1865–1885. Albumen print. Andrew Dickson White Architectural Photographs Collection, Division of Rare and Manuscripts Collections, Cornell University Library.

paneled, portrait-clad walls (fig. 41), then an equally felt presence is the chapels of those same schools (fig. 42), whose antiphonal seating arrangements are echoed in its ascending rows of pew-like benches, facing each other across a central aisle.[45]

Yet the major influence on the room was not academic at all. Wilson had launched his career with a book on *Congressional Government* (1885), which constituted a critique of the American system of checks and balances and advocated the strengths of British parliamentarism. Though he would later moderate his views, he was a scholar—and remained a supporter—of parliamentary government, admiring its capacity for (indeed, encouragement of) topical debate involving all representative parties. What better place, then, on which to model Princeton's new seat of counsel and governance than the British House of Commons (fig. 43)? Appropriately, that space had itself evolved out of churchly origins (it was based on the design of Westminster's St. Stephen's Chapel, where the Commons met for three centuries) and was perfectly suited to promote—and guide—the vigorous but reasoned discourse Wilson envisioned for Princeton's own "Council Chamber." For as Winston Churchill later

Figure 43. *The House Commons*, 1858. Joseph Nash (1808–1878). Gouache. Palace of Westminster Collection.

Figure 44. Faculty Room, east wall. Historical Photograph Collection, University Archives, Department of Rare Books and Special Collections, Princeton University Library.

said with regard to the rebuilding of the British Commons following its wartime destruction, "We shape our buildings; thereafter they shape us." Wilson would doubtless have agreed. Drawing upon American Colonial Revival and English collegiate, religious, and civic interiors, the Faculty Room's architectural references added significantly to the already freighted history of the space. When the portraits were added to the mix, Princeton had created a place of enormously rich symbolic import, a fitting culmination to the many identities the room had assumed over a century and a half of use.[46]

Among the chief satisfactions for Wilson in the Faculty Room's completion must have been the chance it presented to hang a portrait of one of his heroes, George Washington, in a space recalling the arena of another, British Prime Minister William Gladstone. The Washington portrait was installed along the room's eastern wall (fig. 44) and remained there until thirty years later, when the arrival of another, British George occasioned its removal to the southern end wall, flanking the new acquisition (fig. 45). In 1936, several historically minded alumni had made a gift of a portrait of King George II (fig. 46) on the condition it be hung in the Faculty Room, thus restoring to the space an image of the man in some distant sense

responsible for Princeton's existence. A year earlier, members of the same group donated a smaller portrait of King William III, Prince of Orange and Nassau (fig. 47), whose titles had provided the name for the young college and the building comprising it, making him something of a patron saint.[47]

The room's rehanging to accommodate the portraits of Princeton's founding spirits meant not only the unlikely juxtaposition of George the patriot with George the king, but more significantly seems to have provided a new logic for the positioning of the rest of the pictures. Previously, the most recent presidents—McCosh, Patton, Wilson, Hibben—were accorded the prime locations on the wall behind the desk of the sitting president (figs. 36, 44), buttressing current authority by reference to the immediate past. Their replacement with portraits of more venerable figures instead lent a desirably historicized air to that most

Figure 46. *George II, King of England* (1683–1760), ca. 1727–32. Artist unknown; after Sir Godfrey Kneller (1646–1723). Oil on canvas. Gift of members of the Classes of 1894 and 1919.

important end of the room and allowed the remaining presidential images to be arrayed more or less chronologically along the side walls. As a 1947 *Princeton Herald* article explained, "The portraits are arranged in the room in the following order: on the wall opposite the entrance and on the far end of the right side wall are hung portraits of founders and early benefactors, on the side walls are Presidents, and on the end wall are noted alumni" (figs. 48, 49).

Figure 47. *William III, King of England, Prince of Orange and Nassau* (1650–1702). Caspar Netscher (1639–1684). Oil on canvas. Gift of members of the Class of 1894.

While there exists a certain irony in situating portraits of individuals with little more than symbolic institutional affiliation in the place of honor, the effect of the new hanging was to construct Princeton's history organically, as in a family tree, with the founders begetting the early presidents, who yield in turn to the later ones, and the school's progeny—its alumni—proudly exhibited on the back wall (fig. 50). Offering a visual recapitulation of the life of the University, the installation naturalizes the past even as it suggests growth and continuance. By tradition, the image of the incumbent president does not yet appear in the room, which underscores the extenuation of the display and bespeaks its primary concern with the strength of the institution rather than its current leadership—just the opposite of portraiture's more political use.[48]

In the years since the addition of the founders' portraits, little has changed in the Faculty Room, except as paintings of successive presidents gradually swell its ranks (fig. 51). Tables have been placed in the central aisle, about 1940 the vaguely medieval light fixtures were

Figure 48. Faculty Room, south wall.

Figure 49. Faculty Room, west and north walls.

Figure 50. Faculty Room, northeast corner.

Figure 51. *Harold T. Shapiro* (born 1935),
President (1988–2001); 1991. Ron Sherr
(born 1952). Oil and gold leaf on wood panel.

replaced by chandeliers, and the ceiling's toned detail has given way to an even white, altogether lending the room a lighter, more hospitable feel. Yet it remains an imposing place—the result, as far as the portraits are concerned, not so much of their individual grandeur as of their cumulative effect. Most of the paintings in the room are surprisingly modest, though the few heads of state evince a suitable majesty. Much of the quiet power of the space lies in the portraits' collective subsumption of individual identity under the broader mantle of the institutional narrative. The thirty-three portraits lining the walls trace Princeton's trajectory from the small religious school of the mid-eighteenth century to the diverse secular university it is today, just as the room and its varied uses mirror that same evolution. The Faculty Room's thirty-fourth portrait, to be added upon the retirement of Princeton's current president, Shirley M. Tilghman, will break the gender barrier in place from the start, in this way similarly reflecting institutional as well as wider cultural advances.

103

Faculty meetings continue to be held in the room, although for most at the University the space serves primarily as the decorous repository of Princeton's institutional memory. Members of the board of trustees gather in it several times each year to help chart the school's future, perhaps finding in portraits of past trustees sanction for their own activity. But it is through another sort of meeting that the Faculty Room now performs its most important role. Every day, scores of visitors, many of them prospective students, experience the lure of Princeton's history there as part of a campus tour or admission information session. In the hushed room, with "its air of great dignity," as the *Herald* article described it, the predominating sense is of stability and permanence. Surrounded by the University's honored ghosts and aged walls, one feels at the very heart of Princeton.

If paintings can be imagined to have lives of their own, then surely none do so more plausibly than portraits. And few portraits anywhere have had more eventful careers than Peale's *George Washington after the Battle of Princeton*. Unlike other great icons, it has hardly been peripatetic in its long life, and is distinctive in part for the opposite reason: for more than two centuries it hung in today's Faculty Room, a vital part of all the changes there, before exigencies of protection and accessibility necessitated its removal to the Princeton University Art Museum. On the occasion of the exhibition this volume accompanies, the portrait has been returned to its original surroundings, with its famous frame lustrously restored. Its presence brings the visual narrative of Princeton University—multilayered, still unfolding—appropriately back to its beginning.

1. Board of Trustees Minutes and Records, vol. 3, p. 518, University Archives, Department of Rare Books and Special Collections, Princeton University Library (hereafter abbreviated, "Trustees Minutes").

2. The author of the letter in which the "Ornaments of the State" quotation appears is unknown, but internal evidence suggests it was written between 1748 and 1750 by founding trustee Ebenezer Pemberton; see Alexander Leitch, *A Princeton Companion* (Princeton: Princeton University Press, 1978), 199–200. Dickinson quoted in David C. Humphrey, "The Struggle for Sectarian Control of Princeton, 1745–1760," *New Jersey History* 91 (1973): 83.

3. The charters of October 22,1746 (which Princeton celebrates as the date of its founding), and September 14, 1748, are reprinted in Thomas Jefferson Wertenbaker's still serviceable *Princeton, 1746–1896* (Princeton: Princeton University Press, 1946), 396–404, quote from 396. A cogent synopsis of the founding is in Leitch, *Princeton Companion*, 197–200. Also useful is John M. Murrin's long "Introduction" appearing in the final two volumes of the prosopographical series *Princetonians, 1748–1794*, published between 1976 and 1991 under several editors and containing many valuable conclusions about Princeton's early students, including the proportion destined for the ministry and evidence of the school's distinctive ecumenism.

4. The balance of religious and secular education at Princeton, and the school's early history, generally, has been extensively documented and interpreted; in addition to the basic sources cited in the previous note, see in particular Francis L. Broderick, "Pulpit, Physics, and Politics: The Curriculum of the College of New Jersey, 1746–1794," *William and Mary Quarterly* 6, no. 1 (1949): 42–68; Humphrey, "The Struggle for Sectarian Control"; Alison B. Olson, "The Founding of Princeton University: Religion and Politics in Eighteenth-Century New Jersey," *New Jersey History* 87 (1969), 133–50; and especially Mark A. Noll, *Princeton and the Republic, 1768–1822: The Search for a Christian Enlightenment in the Era of Samuel Stanhope Smith* (Princeton: Princeton University Press, 1989).

5. Aaron Burr to William Hogg, December 3, 1755, Aaron Burr Collection, University Archives, Department of Rare Books and Special Collections, Princeton University Library (hereafter abbreviated, "Princeton University Archives"). On the Shippen-Smith design, see Charles E. Peterson, *Robert Smith: Architect, Builder, Patriot, 1722–1777* (Philadelphia: The Athenaeum of Philadelphia, 2000), 45–50. Ezra Stiles noted his initial visit to Princeton in a journal documenting his trip from New Haven to Philadelphia and back in the autumn of 1754, reprinted as "Diary of Ezra Stiles," *Proceedings of the Massachusetts Historical Society*, ser. 2, vol. 7 (1892): 338–344, quoted at 343; Stiles's later sketch is reproduced in F. B. Dexter, *Extracts from the Itineraries and Other Miscellanies of Ezra Stiles* (New Haven: Yale University Press, 1916), 389. The same sketch informs the more detailed plan appearing in Henry Lyttleton Savage, *Nassau Hall, 1756–1956* (Princeton: Princeton University Press, 1956), 17.

6. Gilbert Tennent to Reverend Dr. Guise, November 15, 1757, quoted in Savage, *Nassau Hall*, 15. Samuel Blair, *An Account of the College of New-Jersey* (Woodbridge, N.J.: James Parker, 1764), 12. Ashbel Green's remarks were posthumously reprinted as "Dr. Witherspoon's Administration at Princeton College," *Presbyterian Magazine* 4, no. 10 (1854): 470.

7. For Belcher's donations, see Trustees Minutes, September 24, 1755; and Donald Drew Egbert, *Princeton Portraits* (Princeton: Princeton University Press, 1947), 4. On the portrait of George II, see Egbert, 4, 21–22.

Information on the portraits' locations is gleaned from several sources, notably Blair, *Account*, 12–13. For the eulogy on George II, see Samuel Blair, *An Oration Pronounced at Nassau-Hall, January 14, 1761; On Occasion of the Death of His Late Majesty King George II* (Woodbridge, N.J.: James Parker, 1761), quoted at 6.

8. Egbert, *Princeton Portraits*, 21.

9. On the Battle of Princeton, see Richard M. Ketchum, *The Winter Soldiers: The Battles for Trenton and Princeton* (1973; rpt., New York: Henry Holt, 1999); and David Hackett Fischer, *Washington's Crossing* (New York: Oxford University Press, 2004), 324–45. Historians' skepticism regarding the fate of *George II* is understandable. Describing the incident as "a legend long cherished in the college," David Hackett Fischer has suggested that the painting was "more likely . . . attacked by an American infantryman with bayonet or sword" (*Washington's Crossing*, 339). But the near-contemporary accounts of the trustees and Green do support at least most of the story, although whether it was Hamilton's artillery which fired the fateful shot is unclear. For the trustees' account, see Trustees Minutes, vol. 1, p. 236 (September 25, 1783). Green's recollection is in his "Witherspoon's Administration," 470. As for the Belcher portrait, William A. Dod's *History of the College of New Jersey, from Its Commencement, A.D., 1746, to 1783* (Princeton: J.T. Robinson, 1844), 49, records that this painting was in turn "entirely destroyed by the British soldiery."

10. British troops were known to especially target Presbyterian churches—indeed, some in England called the war the Presbyterian revolt, a not entirely unjust characterization, given that all but one of General Washington's colonels at Yorktown was a Presbyterian elder; see Douglas Wilson, *Five Cities That Ruled the World: How Jerusalem, Athens, Rome, London, and New York Shaped Global History* (Nashville, Tenn.: Thomas Nelson, 2009), 143–47, Walpole quoted at 145. For the Hazard quote, see Fred Shelley, "Ebenezer Hazard's Diary: New Jersey During the Revolution," *Proceedings of the New Jersey Historical Society* 90, no. 3 (1972), 172.

11. Green's description of Nassau Hall's postwar condition is in Noll, *Princeton and the Republic*, 74. For the second Green quote, see his "Witherspoon's Administration," 470. Statistics regarding the political orientation and military service of early alumni are from James McLachlan, *Princetonians, 1748–1768* (Princeton: Princeton University Press, 1976), xxiii.

12. Besides Washington, the other future American president attending commencement was alumnus James Madison, Class of 1771. For a full account of the event, see Varnum Lansing Collins, *The Continental Congress at Princeton* (Princeton: Princeton University Library, 1908), 155–66; also see Anne Gossen, *Princeton, 1783: The Nation's Capital* (Princeton: Morven Museum and Garden, 2009), 41–42. On changes in the curriculum under Witherspoon, see Broderick, "Pulpit, Physics, and Politics." More generally, Noll, *Princeton and the Republic*, discusses the college in the context of what the author terms its "republican Christian Enlightenment" orientation.

13. The new portrait was placed, appropriately enough, on the prayer hall's western wall, opposite the position of the former portrait of George II; see Dod, *College of New Jersey*, 49. For the trustees' commission of the painting, see Trustees Minutes, vol. 1, p. 236 (September 25, 1783); for Washington's response to it, see Egbert, *Princeton Portraits*, 322. Peale quoted in Donald Drew Egbert, "The Nassau Hall Portrait of George Washington Reproduced in Color," *Princeton University Library Chronicle* 8, no. 2 (1947), 60.

14. On Peale and the Philadelphia militia at the Battle of Princeton, see Steven Rosswurm, *Arms, Country, and Class: The Philadelphia Militia and the "Lower Sort" during the American Revolution* (New Brunswick, N.J.: Rutgers University Press, 1987), 130–32.

15. The original *George Washington after the Battle of Princeton* was executed in 1779 and is now at Philadelphia's Pennsylvania Academy of the Fine Arts. Princeton's replica, known as the Wilson-Munn version, dates from a few years later. It was donated to the University in 1924 by Charles Allen Munn, Class of 1881, and hung in the Graduate School and more recently in Firestone Library. In 2006, the Wilson-Munn portrait was installed in the Faculty Room as a replacement for *George Washington at the Battle of Princeton*, which had been removed for safekeeping and enhanced visibility to the Princeton University Art Museum after hanging there for 221 years. For information on both portraits, see my entry on *George Washington at the Battle of Princeton* in *Princeton University Art Museum: Handbook of the Collections* (Princeton: Princeton University Art Museum, 2007), 118–19, from which the current discussion is drawn; also see Egbert, *Princeton Portraits*, 326–28; and John Hill Morgan, *Two Early Portraits of George Washington Painted by Charles Willson Peale* (Princeton: Princeton University Press, 1927). On *George Washington at the Battle of Princeton*, see in addition Charles Coleman Sellers, *Portraits and Miniatures by Charles Willson Peale*, vol. 42, pt. 1 of *Transactions of the American Philosophical Society* (1952), 234–35; and David C. Ward, "Pealing Washington: Art, the Battle of Princeton, and the Creation of a National Culture" in *Record: Princeton University Art Museum* 70 (forthcoming, 2011), ed. Karl Kusserow (issue devoted to American art in Princeton collections). On Peale generally and for biographical and other details relevant to the Battle of Princeton portraits, see Sellers, *Charles Willson Peale* (1947; rpt. New York: Scribner's, 1969).

16. Cutler quoted in Egbert, *Princeton Portraits*, 4.

17. One of the "several paintings" destroyed must have been a new portrait of Governor Belcher, evidently installed by the trustees in the prayer hall to replace the one lost during the Battle of Princeton; see Dod, *College of New Jersey*, 49. For the trustees' response to the fire, see John Maclean, *History of the College of New Jersey, from Its Origins in 1746 to the Commencement of 1854* (Philadelphia: J.B. Lippincott, 1877), vol. 2, 32ff., quoted at 32. For Smith's reaction, see Savage, *Nassau Hall*, 126–27; and Egbert, *Princeton Portraits*, 4.

18. James Carnahan to Charles F. Mercer, August 8, 1802, James Carnahan Collection, Princeton University Archives. For Latrobe's work on Nassau Hall, see Savage, *Nassau Hall*, 27–38.

19. On Princeton during this significant period, see Mark A. Noll's erudite and mutually informative *Princeton and the Republic*, 157–291; "The Founding Era of the College of New Jersey, 1746–1822," 1996 manuscript for unrealized volume "From College to University: Essays on the History of Princeton University," ed. Anthony Grafton and John Murrin, University Archives, Department of Rare Books and Special Collections, Princeton University Library; and "The Princeton Trustees of 1807: New Men and New Directions," *Princeton University Library Chronicle* 41 (Spring 1980): 208–30. Also see Wertenbaker, *Princeton, 1746–1896*, 118–72.

20. Maclean's devotion to Princeton's past is additionally suggested by his production, late in life, of a two-volume history of the college, which, perhaps further reflecting his retrospective orientation, stops more than two decades prior to the date of its publication; see Maclean, *History of the College of New Jersey*. On

nostalgia and its implications, see Eric Hobsbawm and Terence Ranger, eds., *The Invention of Tradition* (New York: Cambridge University Press, 1983); and David Lowenthal, *The Past Is a Foreign Country* (New York: Cambridge University Press, 1985).

21. Rembrandt Peale to John Maclean Jr., April 12, 1826, Maclean Files: Correspondence, Office of the President Records, Princeton University Archives. Also see Samuel F. B. Morse to John Maclean Jr., September 30, 1825, ibid.

22. John Maclean Jr. to Trustees of the College, December 18, 1849, ibid. Information on Brown's collection is from Robert P. Emlen, "Picturing the Worthies: An Introduction to The Brown Portrait Collection," Office of the University Curator, Brown University Center for Digital Initiatives, http://dl.lib.brown.edu/portraits/intro.html (accessed January 20, 2010).

23. Trustees Minutes, vol. 3, p. 511. Trustees Minutes, vol. 3, p. 481. Trustees Minutes, vol. 3, p. 503. "College of New Jersey," *Princeton Whig*, December 13, 1850.

24. Maclean to Trustees, December 18, 1849. On the Chamber of Commerce collection, and for institutional portraiture and its implications, see "Portraiture's Use, and Disuse, at the Chamber of Commerce and Beyond," in Karl Kusserow, *Picturing Power: Portraiture and the New York Chamber of Commerce* (New York: Columbia University Press, forthcoming 2011). For the mid-century professionalization of museum and collecting practice, see Joel J. Orosz, *Curators and Culture: The Museum Movement in America, 1740–1870* (Tuscaloosa: University of Alabama Press, 1990), 140–79. The emergence of comprehensive ordering discourses and their relation to collecting are discussed in Susan M. Pearce, *On Collecting: An Investigation into Collecting in the European Tradition* (London: Routledge, 1995), 132.

25. On mid-century Americans' feelings of increased remove from their past, see John Higham, *From Boundlessness to Consolidation: The Transformation of American Culture, 1848–1860* (Ann Arbor: William L. Clements Library, 1969), 18; and Orosz, *Curators and Culture*, 182–83.

26. "Nassau Hall in Ruins," *New-York Daily Times*, March 14, 1855. Also see the *Princeton Press* broadside, "Nassau Hall Burnt Down!!," March 12, 1855.

27. *Princeton Press* quoted in Robert C. Smith, "John Notman's Nassau Hall," *Princeton University Library Chronicle* 14, no. 3 (1953), 111. Notman's selection to renovate Nassau Hall made sense, and not just because he was Scottish; he had recently designed perhaps the town's three grandest residences (one of which, Prospect, later served as the home of Princeton's president, and another of which, Lowrie House, currently does); see Constance M. Greiff, *John Notman, Architect, 1810–1865* (Philadelphia: The Athenaeum of Philadelphia, 1979). Notman's drawings for Nassau Hall do not survive, but the "plan & elevation" referenced in his initial letter to Maclean about the project details a "Hall or Picture Gallery" over the library, "lighted from the roof"; see John Notman to John Maclean Jr., March 22, 1855, John Maclean Jr. Letters, Office of the President Records, Princeton University Archives. For the Building Committee's description, see Trustees Minutes, vol. 4, p. 172 (June 27, 1860). The final quotation is from an earlier report of the same committee; see Report of the Building Committee, June 1855, John Maclean Jr. Letters, Office of the President Records, Princeton University Archives.

28. Report of President James McCosh, Trustees Minutes, vol. 5, p. 27 (December 16, 1868). The Sibley anecdote is recorded in James McLachlan, "The *Choice of Hercules*: American Student Societies in the Early 19th

Century," in *The University in Society*, ed. Lawrence Stone, vol. 2, *Europe, Scotland, and the United States from the 16th to the 20th Century* (Princeton: Princeton University Press, 1974), 471.

29. Prior to Witherspoon's application of the term "campus," from the Latin for "field," to pastoral Princeton, the grounds of American colleges were called yards, as still at Harvard, and in the more general "school-yard"; see Leitch, *Princeton Companion*, 74–75.

30. John Maclean Jr., "Inventory of Portraits for a Campus Gallery" (ca. 1868), Maclean Files: Correspondence, Office of the President Records, Princeton University Archives. "Trustee Minutes on the President's Report" (December 18, 1860), Office of the President Records, Princeton University Archives. The trustees' fifty dollar appropriation ultimately yielded Edward Ludlow Mooney's *Matthew Boyd Hope* (1861), a bust-length portrait painted from a photograph.

31. McCosh quoted in James McCosh, *The Life of James McCosh: A Record Chiefly Autobiographical*, ed. William Milligan Sloane (New York: Scribner's, 1896), 196. Egbert, *Princeton Portraits*, 6, records his statement about the presidential portraits. For Green's investigation of Smith, see Wertenbaker, *Princeton, 1746–1896*, 121–22. Green apparently really was much the benevolent figure his portrait portrays; the point here is that this is *all* the portrait conveys.

32. *Yale Literary Magazine* quoted in Scott Casper, *Constructing American Lives: Biography and Culture in Nineteenth-Century America* (Chapel Hill: University of North Carolina Press, 1999), 1. Carlyle quoted in Marcia Pointon, *Hanging the Head: Portraiture and Social Formation in Eighteenth-Century England* (New Haven: Yale University Press, 1993), 277. The imbrication of history, biography, and portraiture had its roots in the mid-eighteenth century, when James Granger's *Biographical History of England* (1769) combined the three, establishing an epistemology in which biography and its visual correlative portraiture could be systematized into a coherent national history, and more generally into a discourse through which the past could be ordered to make sense of the present. Such a system, it was felt, and as Carlyle later claimed, would provide a view into "the very marrow of the world's history" through the lives—and countenances—of those deemed to have effected it. The appearance in this country of James Herring and James Barton Longacre's *National Portrait Gallery of Distinguished Americans* (published, at first serially, beginning in 1833), along with numerous successors like William H. Brown's *Portrait Gallery of Distinguished American Citizens* (1845) and Charles Lester Edwards' *Gallery of Illustrious Americans* (1850) indicates the appeal here of similarly structuring the past through the complementary mediums of portraiture and biography. On the general use of biography to constitute history, see Casper, *Constructing American Lives*; for its relationship to portraiture, see Marcia Pointon, *Hanging the Head*, esp. 53–78 and, on the formation of England's National Portrait Gallery, 227–44.

33. George Wilson, ed., *Portrait Gallery of the Chamber of Commerce of the State of New-York: Catalogue and Biographical Sketches* (New York: Press of the Chamber of Commerce, 1890), vi. Twenty-three portraits by Mooney eventually entered Princeton's collection. The artist returned the favor of Maclean's repeated patronage, painting him once in 1850 (fig. 19) and again in 1873, both comparatively sensitive efforts. Little known today though evidently successful in his lifetime, Mooney was an inveterate copyist, beginning his career with six renditions of his teacher Henry Inman's portrait of Martin Van Buren; see *Appleton's Cyclopaedia of American Biography* (1888), s.v. "Mooney, Edward Ludlow." The source for the Davies portrait is recorded on the back of the canvas. Quality later did come more to the fore in Princeton's collecting

practice, when John White Alexander was introduced to the school as a drawing instructor, which led to several excellent portraits.

34. The intention to orient the Princeton exhibit around history was announced in "Princeton's Exhibit at the World's Fair," *The Daily Princetonian*, February 14, 1893. For the *Princeton Press*'s extensive impressions, see "Princeton at the Fair" in the September 2, 1893, issue. On the contemporary appeal of historical portraiture, see Richard H. Saunders, "The Eighteenth-Century Portrait in American Culture of the Nineteenth and Twentieth Centuries," in *The Portrait in Eighteenth-Century America*, ed. Ellen G. Miles (Newark: University of Delaware Press, 1993), 138–52, esp. 140–42; on period nostalgia, see the sources cited in note 20 above; and for antimodernism, see T. J. Jackson Lears, *No Place of Grace: Antimodernism and the Transformation of American Culture, 1880–1920* (Chicago: University of Chicago Press, 1981).

35. In his inaugural address, McCosh had laid out his expansive vision for the college, which he believed must become, as one scholar put it, "more than a collegiate expression of the Presbyterian denomination"; see J. David Hoeveler Jr., *James McCosh and the Scottish Intellectual Tradition: From Glasgow to Princeton* (Princeton: Princeton University Press, 1981), quoted at 218. For the address itself, see *Inauguration of James McCosh, D.D., LL.D., as President of the College of New Jersey* (New York: Robert Carter and Brothers, 1868), 35–96. On the new museum, see Sara E. Turner, "The E.M. Museum: Building and Breaking an Interdisciplinary Collection," *Princeton University Library Chronicle* 65, no. 2 (2004): 237–63. As Turner notes (p. 252), the establishment of the E.M. Museum coincided with the development of a second Museum of Natural History at the newly completed School of Science. The "wandering" history of Princeton's old museum was described in the "Olla-podrida" column of the *Nassau Literary Magazine*'s issue of April 1874 (n.p.). The *Princetonian* described the new museum in its January 16, 1879, issue. As was later revealed, the museum received funding from William Libbey, who named it after his wife, Elizabeth Marsh, and whose son, William Libbey Jr., Class of 1877, eventually oversaw it, following Guyot's retirement. Guyot quoted in *The Princeton Book: A Series of Sketches Pertaining to the History, Organization and Present Condition of the College of New Jersey* (Boston: Houghton, Osgood, 1879), 265.

36. On the general development of American museums, and for a discussion of the changing balance between education and professional interests in them, see Orosz, *Curators and Culture*. Information on Rhode Island Hall is from Joukowsky Institute for Archaeology and the Ancient World, "The Transformation of Rhode Island Hall," ch. 3, "History of Rhode Island Hall," http://proteus.brown.edu/rihalltransform/6996 (accessed January 20, 2010).

37. Guyot's habit of referring to the museum as a Synoptic Room is described in an unpublished 1884 manuscript, "The Life and Scientific Work of Arnold Guyot" (p. 48), prepared by his protégé, William Libbey Jr. (Department of Rare Books and Special Collections, Manuscript Division, Princeton University Library); Guyot quoted in Turner, "E.M. Museum," 237. The museum was constituted in the midst of the great debate on evolutionary theory, recapitulating the era's larger discussion about the proper relationship of science and religion, in which Princeton's intellectuals staked out an unexpectedly wide range of positions considering the school's religious orientation. In 1865, the college apparently aimed to tackle the issue head-on with the appointment of Reverend Charles Woodruff Shields to a professorship in the "harmony of religion and revealed science." Surprisingly, McCosh announced himself a Darwinian, reasoning that the theory was not a

denial of God but a manifestation of God's unfolding plan. Of instruction at the college, generally, he noted, "We do not subject religion to science; but we are equally careful not to subject science to religion. . . . When a scientific theory is brought to us, our first inquiry is not whether it is consistent with religion, but whether it is true" (McCosh, *Life of James McCosh*, 233); also see Hoeveler, *James McCosh*; and, more generally, George S. Marsden, *The Soul of the American University* (New York: Oxford University Press, 1996).

38. Hawkins's anti-Darwinian views accorded with those of Guyot (expressed in his *Creation* of 1884) in supporting the notion of limited evolution under God's plan without accepting the theory of natural selection. For McCosh, by contrast, natural selection was but a facet of an overarching intelligent design. Both points of view were accommodated in the museum, whose displays, while clearly evolutionary in the sense of showing progression over time, did not specifically advocate "evolution" as Darwin theorized the term. For information on the Hawkins paintings, see Valerie Bramwell and Robert M. Peck, *All in the Bones: A Biography of Benjamin Waterhouse Hawkins* (Philadelphia: Academy of Natural Sciences, 2008), 85–89. As the Mercury statue suggests, the E.M. Museum also contained the college's then small and indifferent collection of art, which in 1890 was moved into the new Museum of Historic Art that McCosh had long advocated; see Betsy Rosasco, "The Teaching of Art and the Museum Tradition at the College of New Jersey: Joseph Henry to Allan Marquand," *Record of The Art Museum, Princeton University* 55, nos. 1–2 (1996): 7–52. Tellingly, the portraits remained in their historic location in Nassau Hall, again underscoring their primary function not as art but as totems of institutional memory.

39. The trustees are quoted in Egbert, *Princeton Portraits*, 69. McCosh introduced graduate fellowships in 1869 and instituted a regular graduate department in 1877. During his presidency, faculty grew from sixteen to forty members, and the student population rose from 250 to more than 600. It was in 1886 that McCosh formally requested the college be named Princeton University.

40. On Wilson at Princeton, see James Axtell, *The Making of Princeton University: From Woodrow Wilson to the Present* (Princeton: Princeton University Press, 2006); and especially W. Barksdale Maynard, *Woodrow Wilson: Princeton to the Presidency* (New Haven: Yale University Press, 2008), in which see 96–109 on the preceptorial system. Wilson's inaugural address is reprinted in *The Papers of Woodrow Wilson,* ed. Arthur S. Link (Princeton: Princeton University Press, 1972), vol. 14, 170–85, quoted at 170, 185.

41. Committee on Grounds and Buildings Minutes, 1904–1905, University Archives, Department of Rare Books and Special Collections, Princeton University Library. *Princeton Alumni Weekly*, November 4, 1905, 84. Raleigh Colston Gildersleeve to Moses Taylor Pyne, June 20, 1905, in *The Papers of Woodrow Wilson,* ed. Arthur S. Link (Princeton: Princeton University Press, 1973), vol. 16, 144–45. The relative costs involved in the Faculty Room's creation are stated in Gildersleeve to Woodrow Wilson, July 8, 1905, and Gildersleeve to Wilson, August 23, 1905, in Link, *Papers of Woodrow Wilson*, vol. 16, 152–53, 182–83. "The New Faculty Room," *Daily Princetonian*, October 7, 1905, reprinted in Link, *Papers of Woodrow Wilson*, vol. 16, 190–91.

42. Cleveland quoted in "The Opening of the New Faculty Room," *Princeton Alumni Weekly*, November 10, 1906. For Wilson's speech, see "Notes for a Talk at the Opening of the Faculty Room in Nassau Hall," in Link, *Papers of Woodrow Wilson*, vol. 16, 479. "Nassau Hall," *Architecture* 24, no. 3 (1911): 129.

43. For information on Harvard's Faculty Room, see Andrea Shen, "History Springs to Life in Restored Faculty Room," *Harvard University Gazette*, February 1, 2001. On Sayles Hall, see Emlen, "Picturing the Worthies." For

the Chamber of Commerce's Great Hall, see Kusserow, *Picturing Power*. And for the (no longer extant) Faculty Room in Dartmouth's Parkhurst Hall, see "Notes toward a Catalog of the Buildings and Landscapes of Dartmouth College," www.dartmo.com/buildings/lmnopbldg.html#parkhursthall (accessed February 3, 2010).

44. Gildersleeve to Wilson, August 24, 1905, in Link, *Papers of Woodrow Wilson*, vol. 16, 182–83. "Nassau Hall," *Architecture*, 129. Information on Drumthwacket from Drumthwacket Foundation, www.drumthwacket.org/history.html (accessed March 2, 2010). For the Colonial Revival, see Richard Guy Wilson, Shaun Eyring, and Kenny Marotta, *Re-creating the American Past: Essays on the Colonial Revival* (Charlottesville: University of Virginia, 2006).

45. On Wilson in England, see Maynard, *Woodrow Wilson*, 40–41, 54–55, letter quoted at 54; also see 83–95 for Princeton's Gothicization and Wilson's role in it.

46. That the Faculty Room is modeled on the House of Commons is a truism of both Princeton history and even the most casual visual analysis, yet explicit contemporary documentation is scarce. The *Princeton Alumni Weekly* for October 6, 1906, stated in describing the space that, "the faculty are to be seated in long benches on the sides of the room facing each other, after the manner of the seating of the House of Commons," but failed to provide more specific information. Of course it makes perfect sense, given Wilson's predilections. Indeed, the reference to the House of Commons, a site a conference and debate, is of a piece with Wilson's preceptorial system, which similarly sought to engender discussion through its promotion by institutional means. For discussing with me the architecture of the British space—its history, form, and the effects of each on parliamentary governance—as well as its particular appeal to Wilson, I am grateful to Mark L. Stout. Churchill's comment was made in a speech delivered October 28, 1944.

47. For the portraits of George II and William III, see Egbert, *Princeton Portraits*, 13–15 and 21–22, respectively; also see, on the donation of the former, Alexander Benson to Matthew C. Fleming, December 18, 1935, Princeton Portrait Files, Princeton University Art Museum.

48. "Portraits of Presidents and Famous Alumni Line Walls of Faculty Room in Nassau Hall," *Princeton Herald*, June 20, 1947. The portraits' genealogical aspect is accentuated by the actual ties of kinship among the early sitters: for example, Aaron Burr was succeeded as president by his father-in-law, Jonathan Edwards; John Witherspoon's tenure preceded that of his son-in-law, Samuel Stanhope Smith; Benjamin Rush (who also appears in Peale's *George Washington at the Battle of Princeton*) was the nephew of founder and president Samuel Finley.

THE GHOST(S) OF THE PAST
HISTORICAL WOUNDS AND "OLD NASSAU"

EDDIE S. GLAUDE JR.

[I]n that protest which each considerate person makes against the superstition of his times, he repeats step for step the part of old reformers, and in the search after truth finds, like them, new perils to virtue.

—Ralph Waldo Emerson, "History"

In great pain and terror one begins to assess the history which has placed one where one is and formed one's point of view.

—James Baldwin, "White Man's Guilt"

The burdens of history can weigh you down. They can place upon your shoulders, if you are attentive to these matters, all of the tragedies and triumphs, hopes and aspirations of a people. Like ghosts they cling to you, shadowing your every move and reminding you in a familiar, haunting cadence, of loss and responsibility.[1] Such burdens can indeed define the trajectory of your life; the myriad problems that have so preoccupied those who have come before you give shape to the difficult task of answering the questions of who am I, how did I come to be? What shall I make of the life around me? Indeed history offers and, in some cases, *imposes* answers; history takes on a sense of fate as if somehow its purported laws and its subsequent course have been set and we are mere pawns moved in some endgame. We find ourselves living within an inheritance that all too often robs us of the chance to forge a distinctive life apart from the questions and problems that set the tone of our people's archive.

It could not be otherwise, or so it would seem, for America's black folk. We are a people, a distinctly modern people, whose very existence depends upon the shattering of histories. The horrors of the slave trade left catastrophe in its wake, separating families and lining the Atlantic Ocean with the souls of millions while Europe, or those nations that would become

Europe, discovered the significance of history to its own self-conception. In the dark holds of slave ships, the terror of black history was unleashed, in which the seemingly unending apprehension of being captured and profoundly wounded established the contours of a people's reclamation of historical presence. "Some who eat nasty themselves," Toni Morrison writes of the middle passage in *Beloved*:

> *I do not eat the men without skin bring us their morning water to drink we have none at night I cannot see the dead man on my face daylight comes through the cracks and I can see his locked eyes . . . we are all trying to leave our bodies behind the man on my face has done it it is hard to make yourself die forever*

Amid unimaginable pain and suffering, history became the place where sorrow, death, *and* possibility came together; its terror resided in its perpetual haunting and its *absolute* necessity, framing the choices, beliefs, and actions of a people caught in and captured by the illusions and failed promises of a fragile experiment in democracy.

Such a view of history foregrounds what the postcolonial theorist, Dipesh Chakrabarty, calls "historical wounds," that sometimes volatile mixture of history and memory. Historical wounds are the consequence, a deadly collateral effect one might say, of the failure to recognize the dignity and standing of "others" within multicultural societies.[2] But for Chakrabarty, the acknowledgment of the wound, particularly by those who have been wounded, occasions the possibility of recovery, historically and personally. "To be able to speak thus—that is, to speak self-consciously from within a history of having been wounded—is itself a historical phenomenon."[3] In short, memory *works* on history, opening spaces for creative action in the shadows of ghastly acts, both past and present, by casting the whole lot into the messiness of experience.[4]

Historical wounds affect the way we orient ourselves to the past. They are not historical truths and yet require those truths as a precondition for their enunciation. That "voicing," in conversation with others, makes the wound public—subject to acknowledgment and/or rejection. As such, historical wounds are not fixed and unchanging; they are open to contestation especially as the social consensus, if one happens to exist, around them changes. For Chakrabarty, historical wounds often pose a serious challenge to the discipline of history; they constitute a critical site for political action based in a deeply felt "experience" made visible by the public workings of memory on the past.[5]

Certainly, historical wounds can be thought of at the level of collective groups or peoples, but equally compelling are the various ways those histories, national histories one might say, shadow individual efforts to forge distinctive selves in light of the histories and memories that haunt, both constraining *and* making possible what can best be thought of, at least in the American context, as an Emersonian preoccupation with self-creation.[6] This is particularly the case in those moments when countries or institutions perform ritualized acts of piety that recall, even without explicitly mentioning it, the occasion of the wound.[7] Chakrabarty rightly notes that the acknowledgment of the wound by those who were in fact the purveyors of the injury contributes to the social consensus that enables the wound itself to impact the way we see, understand, and write about the past. He fails to note, however, that even within periods of relative consensus about historical wounds, public performances of national or institutional piety often re-injure by reminding the wounded of their forced absence from a celebrated and all-too-often blanched past.[8]

This essay occasions an opportunity to reflect on what can be called an Emersonian problematic *with a difference*: to think about the prerogatives of history and the demands of the present in light of the deep wounds of a racial past that shape and condition the choices we make. Like Emerson, my concern, in part, is not so much with how history is written as with how it ought to be read. I commend such an Emersonian view, only colored with the insights of James Baldwin's reflections on the terror of African American history and its place in self-creation. I take up this fraught subject in the context of a unique moment in the history of Princeton University, as it performs a public ritual of piety in formally exhibiting its Faculty Room, adorned with portraits of its esteemed founders, leaders, and alumni (all white males). The back story, I suppose, to this moment is my own fitful navigation of the University's past and present—the fact that I stand, as the portraits in the Faculty Room make glaringly clear, among a host of "latecomers."

I have had the pleasure to teach some amazing students during my time at Princeton. Many have become teachers in urban schools. And every now and again I receive a phone call: they have traveled with their students to Princeton and want me to say a few words to them. More often than not the conversation takes place in the Faculty Room—a space, despite its significance, I rarely experience. It is in the queer juxtaposition of bright-eyed African American children, daring to dream that one day they too will attend Princeton, and the history embodied in the room itself, with its portraits of past presidents and its materiality of exclusion, that I struggle with the complex relation of history and memory. I talk about their futures and challenge them to dream dreams some deem impossible for them, even as they fail to see, besides me, anyone or anything that might reflect them. And yet . . . their aspirations (and sounds) give fresh life to the Faculty Room, lending a countervailing, living materiality to a different iteration of Princeton marked by their very presence at that moment . . . in that space.

The question arises, how does one affiliate with an institution whose history necessarily excludes you? Or, does one ever feel a sense of belonging in a place whose past reminds you, every now and again, of your latecomer status? I do not mean simply the lack of color or the absence of women on the Faculty Room's walls. It could not be otherwise; history declares it so. Instead, the assembled portraits occasion some reflection, at least a moment's pause, on the difficulty of belonging *to* or being *in* a place that must acknowledge, however obliquely, the problems of its past. The issue at hand, then, is not so much about the pictures as such or about Princeton's perceived failure in the past to question its unabashed whiteness and maleness. The issue was and remains about *my* relation to this place, and how that relation complicates, if not undermines, any easy embrace of "Old Nassau" and its alumni of distinction.

For most of Princeton's history people who look like me were not allowed to walk its hallowed halls, and that fact has resulted in a difficult relationship between this extraordinary institution and its African American alumni. Of course, African American students forge life-long bonds while here; they fall in love and experience heartbreak; they enjoy some classes and endure others. In this sense, Princeton will always have a special place in the hearts of its black graduates. But one would be hard pressed to say that these experiences, which would ordinarily generate loyalty and fidelity to the place that made them possible, result in a sense of belonging and possession among most of Princeton's African American alumni. In some ways, so the story is told, these wonderful experiences occur *in spite* of Princeton and reflect, in some sense, a wager: that the stark reality of Princeton's past and the undeniable difficulty of its lived present can be transformed by the possibilities of a not-so-distant future represented, much like the children in the Faculty Room, by our very presence here.

Princeton now has a significant body of alumni of color and we contribute to the overall vitality of the University. This might suggest that Princeton's history ought not to condemn it, especially in the minds and hearts of its graduates, to some irredeemable and shadowy place. Indeed, the presence of all latecomers loudly proclaims a different Princeton. But this takes me back to the awkward moment of recognition: the moment marked by my inability to reconcile the Princeton represented in the Faculty Room and the Princeton of my experiences.

In noting the startling disjunction between "Old Nassau" and the Princeton of today, I neither congratulate the University on a finished job well done nor do I condemn a past that is one of significant accomplishment. Too often when we assess ourselves against the past, we stand in a self-congratulatory mood, patting ourselves on the shoulder for escaping the sins of our mothers and fathers. We tell ourselves stories about our journey to where we are that habitually leave in place blind spots that exclude and deeply hurt others. Too often institutional acts of piety, like neat and tidy national histories, leave the margins invisible—filling the room with toxins that harm the soul; and latecomers, not all but most, retreat into the safety of their own rooms to find space to breathe only to change into some ghastly figure, like Kafka's Gregor Samsa, unhoused in what they imagined to be their own home.

Something more fundamental must happen if we are to avoid this fate. We must encounter the fullness of our history, and that requires a more intense encounter with who we take ourselves to be. James Baldwin made this point about America in general—that the myth of its innocence shields the nation from the brutal facts of its past—and his relentless attention to the blind spots constituted, at least for him, a constraint on American hubris and enabled a qualified embrace of a nation that resolutely rejected him. Writing in the early 1960s, Baldwin grappled intensely with the difficult task of conceiving of a robust sense of black individuality in the context of a nation still committed to white supremacy *and* to the notion of an "uncontaminated innocence" (a young Emerson's words). The illusion of innocence concealed (and conceals) the darkness in America's soul. As Baldwin makes explicit, "It is the innocence which constitutes the crime."[9]

For Baldwin, an intimate understanding of the centrality of black folk in the illusion of America's innocence was necessary if we are to break loose from the stranglehold of America's past. Like Emerson, he urged us to read history and its meanings in order to discover how it might serve us in the present. But unlike Emerson, Baldwin's intimacy with the destruction wrought by white supremacy—his wounds—framed his reflections about the constraints of history and the possibilities made available to us by our appropriate reading of it.

History and how we invoke it matters a great deal, and I see exploring and communicating this truth to be a central part of my mission here. As Baldwin writes, "the great force of history comes from the fact that we carry it within us, are unconsciously controlled by it in many ways, and history is literally *present* in all that we do. It could scarcely be otherwise, since it is to history that we owe our frames of reference, our identities, and our aspirations."[10] To recognize history's presence in us is to understand the absolute necessity of fingering its jagged edges, as I do here in this essay, in order—if just for a moment—to prick our frames of reference and to unsettle our established identities. For Baldwin, and for me, the past orients us appropriately to the tasks of self-creation and of reconstructing American society. And here we return to one of the quotations that begins this essay:

> *In great pain and terror one begins to assess the history which has placed one where one is and formed one's point of view. In great pain and terror because, therefore, one enters into battle with that historical creation, Oneself, and attempts to recreate oneself according to a principle more humane and more liberating; one begins the attempt to achieve a level of personal maturity and freedom which robs history of its tyrannical power, and also changes history.*[11]

These words provide a blueprint for addressing the challenge of "Old Nassau." Princeton's latecomers ought not to discard the past. It is what it is. And we understand all too well its charm and magic. We must face this institution's history in all of its complexity and see how its imprint informs and shapes our choices. Confronting it allows us, at least for a moment, to break loose from "its tyrannical power" so that we may imagine ourselves and the University anew.

History's ghosts occasion an opportunity to reflect on the difficulty of belonging. How we manage that difficulty involves how we orient ourselves to the problem. In the end, I accept Princeton's past as I do America's, not out of uncomplicated reverence, but because of an unyielding faith in future possibilities demonstrated by our presence here today. Princeton is a place where memory can work on history to open up space—an ultimate act of creation—not only for those young black and brown children dreaming in the Faculty Room, but also for all of us who struggle to forge a distinctive life illuminated by the wounded lives already lived. We turn to the past, then, to better equip ourselves to invade the future intelligently and with love.

Participants in black alumni conference, "Coming Back and Moving Forward," on Blair Arch steps, 2009. Office of Communications, Princeton University.

1. Here I am drawing on the work of Walter Benjamin. For Benjamin, "the true image of the past flits by," and the past and the future are connected through spectral relays because the "dead become ghosts." I am also deeply indebted to Toni Morrison's view of history in her novel *Beloved* (1987). See Benjamin's *Iluminations*, ed. Hannah Arendt, trans. Harry Zohn (New York: Shocken, 1968). Also see his *Selected Writings*, vol. 1: 1913–1926, ed. Marcus Bullock and Michael Jennings (Cambridge: Harvard University Press, 1996), 43–83.

2. Dipesh Chakrabarty, "History and the Politics of Recognition," in *Manifestos for History,* ed. Keith Jenkins, Sue Morgan, and Alun Munslow (London: Routledge, 2007), 77–87. Chakrabarty's discussion of historical wounds is indebted to Charles Taylor's account of the politics of recognition. See Taylor's "The Politics of Recognition," in *Multiculturalism: Examining the Politics of Recognition,* ed. Amy Gutman (Princeton: Princeton University Press, 1994), 25–74.

3. Chakrabarty, "History and the Politics of Recognition," 77.

4. I offer an account of the importance of experience, pragmatically understood, in "Agency, Slavery, and African American Christianity," in my book, *In a Shade of Blue: Pragmatism and the Politics of Black America* (Chicago: University of Chicago Press, 2007), 89–111.

5. See Chakrabarty, "History and the Politics of Recognition," 77–79.

6. See Stanley Cavell, *Conditions Handsome and Unhandsome: The Constitution of Emersonian Perfectionism* (Chicago: University of Chicago Press, 1990).

7. I understand piety, following George Santayana and John Dewey, as an explicit acknowledgment of indebtedness to the sources of one's being. Or, to use the work of Michael Roth: "Piety is the turning of oneself so as to be in relation to the past, to experience oneself as coming after. . . .This is the attempt at fidelity to (not correspondence with) the past." See Roth, *The Ironist's Cage: Memory, Trauma, and the Construction of History* (New York: Columbia University Press, 1995), 16.

8. When Americans, for example, celebrate Independence Day, they all too often forget the uneasy relation of African Americans to that moment. I am reminded of Frederick Douglass's oration of July 5, 1852, when he challenged the illusion of America as a beacon light of freedom with the condemning question, "What to the Slave is the 4th of July?" Even with a social consensus about slavery as wrong, the national commemorative calendar still contains ritual moments that are blind to the wound. The Fourth of July remains an unabashed celebration of the grandeur of the American project (Douglass's ghost rarely haunts it). As such, and perhaps this has changed with the election of Barack Obama, many African Americans have a different orientation to the holiday—a day off and a day for barbecue, not a moment for the expression of patriotism.

9. Baldwin's forceful observation was delivered in the context of a letter written to his nephew, which attempted to account for the wounded character of his brother, his nephew's father: "I know what the world has done to my brother and how narrowly he has survived it. And I know, which is much worse, and this is the crime of which I accuse my country and my countrymen, and for which neither I nor time nor history will ever forgive them, that they have destroyed and are destroying hundreds of thousands of

lives and do not know it and do not want to know it. One can be, indeed one must strive to become, tough and philosophical concerning destruction and death, for this is what most of mankind has been best at since we have heard of man. (But remember: most of mankind is not all of mankind). But it is not permissible that the authors of devastation should also be innocent. It is the innocence which constitutes the crime." See James Baldwin, "My Dungeon Shook," in *Collected Essays*, ed. Toni Morrison (New York: Library of America, 1998), 292.

10. James Baldwin, "White Man's Guilt," in *The Price of the Ticket: Collected Nonfiction, 1948–1985* (New York: St. Martin's, 1985), 410.

11. Ibid.

THE INNER SANCTUM

From this Holy of Holies where McCosh and Maclean
preside over us, each from his little shelf,
where they join forces with Bowen, Goheen,
Witherspoon and Wilson, where Washington himself

threatens to spur
us into action on the serried gray and red tile
while Dickinson and Burr
might yet have us cross the aisle

with William III, the Prince of Orange and Nassau
(whose name to an Irish Catholic was not without taint
but, since relations have begun to thaw,
a not unlikely "patron saint"),

we march out under the banner Princeton has unfurled
from this Holy of Holies to the whole world.

—PAUL MULDOON

Photography Credits

Cover: Bruce M. White

Page 4: Bruce M. White

Page 6: Denise Applewhite, Office of Communications, Princeton University

Pages 11-12: Bruce M. White

Morrison: Frontispiece, figs. 1–3: Bruce M. White

Wilentz: Frontispiece: Historical Photograph Collection, University Archives, Department of Rare Books and Special Collections, Princeton University Library, photo George K. Warren; page 45: John Jameson, Office of Communications, Princeton University

Kusserow: Frontispiece, figs. 2, 4, 7, 8, 10–15, 17–21, 24–26, 34, 35, 46–51; p. 105: Bruce M. White; figs. 9, 16: Jeffrey Evans

Glaude: Frontispiece: Bruce M. White; p. 121: Evelyn Tu, Office of Communications, Princeton University

Muldoon: Frontispiece: Bruce M. White